Neighboring

Jorge Acevedo

Elaine A. Heath
General Editor

HOLY LIVING: NEIGHBORING

ISBN 9781501877605

Manufactured in the United States of America

19 20 21 22 23 24 25 26 27 28—10 9 8 7 6 5 4 3 2 1

ABINGDON PRESS

Nashville

TABLE OF CONTENTS

DEDICATION

To my "Jenga" Covenant Group

Dale Locke, Matthew Hartsfield, Max Wilkins, Wayne Wiatt, Doug Kokx, and Joe MacLaren

For almost thirty years, you have been my "band of brothers." Together, we have walked through the valleys of despair, disappointment, and discouragement. Together, we have forged the rivers of addiction, affliction, and adversity. Together, we have walked the paths of change, conflict, and chaos. And together, we have scaled the mountains of rejoicing, redemption, and reconciliation. You have been my best neighbors in this gift of life and ministry, and you have helped me experience the grace and mercy of our neighboring Savior and Friend, Jesus. Thank you. I dedicate this book to each of you for your invaluable and irreplaceable friendship.

FOREWORD

From the time that individuals began responding to Jesus' call to follow him, they began to learn rhythms of life that would be essential for them to be able to live their lives wholeheartedly for God. Chief among these practices was prayer. Jesus modeled for them how to withdraw from busy service to spend time alone in prayer. He offered prayer verbally in front of them, and when they asked, taught them to pray with the prayer we now call the Lord's Prayer. Following Jesus' ascension, as the disciples waited in Jerusalem "for what the Father had promised," that is, the Holy Spirit, Luke tells us that "all were united in their devotion to prayer" (Acts 1:4, 14). Prayer was foundational and formational, positioning them to receive the Holy Spirit, God's empowering presence that both indwelled and propelled them.

Following that transformative event, in due time they followed the Spirit's leading and bore witness to Jesus "to the end of the earth" (Acts 1:8). Their lives were busy, on the move, teaching, preaching, healing, explaining, encouraging, and confronting the evil and injustice of their society. Yet all of that doing, they knew, had to emanate from a deeply grounded experience of being. Nurturing a loving relationship with God was a central commitment that they, like we, had to learn to practice. Apart from this relationship, their busyness was meaningless. So they and those who followed them in the faith added to the practice of prayer a wide range of spiritual disciplines to strengthen their relationship with God, help them grow in Christlikeness, and fuel them for the work God called them to do.

Some of these practices—things like meditation, simplicity, and fasting—are more inwardly focused. Others are expressed outwardly and corporately— things like confession, worship, and celebration. And some of the practices can be both, such as prayer. All of them—and there are many—work together to help us achieve lives of balance, anchored securely to Christ and equipped for meaningful engagement with others.

This book is one in a series of eight, each of which focuses on a single practice or discipline. In this volume, Jorge Acevedo calls us back to that which Jesus said was most important: loving God completely and loving our neighbors as we love ourselves. I invite you to expand your understanding and your practice of what Jesus' call to us means.

Elaine A. Heath,
General Editor

INTRODUCTION
Won't You Be My Neighbor?

In 2018, the delightful movie *Won't You Be My Neighbor?* was a surprise hit. The documentary explores the life of Fred Rogers, an ordained Presbyterian minister and the beloved host of the PBS children's show *Mr. Rogers' Neighborhood*. Every episode of the show began the same way as Fred opened the door and began to sing: "It's a beautiful day in this neighborhood . . . ."[1]

Then the kind and lovable host would walk down the steps to a closet where he would remove his work jacket and put on a comfy sweater, followed by a quick stroll over to a bench where he would take off his dress shoes and put on some cozy sneakers. It was all so soothing, so calming, so reassuring.

Mr. Rogers' Neighborhood has a simple message: everyone, especially children, is worthy of love and everyone has the capacity to love. It's that simple. Love yourself and love others. For thirty-three years, this follower of Jesus invited the most vulnerable among us to join him in the Neighborhood of Make-believe with his friends X the Owl, Queen Sara Saturday, and King Friday. There, kids could discover the power of love. Interestingly, Rev. Rogers never served as pastor of a local church, but the Presbyterian Church asked Fred to serve as a minister to children through television and media.[2] They were his flock, and he was their pastor.

This little book is about loving our neighbors. Both the Old and New Testament challenge the people of God to love God completely and to love our neighbors as we love ourselves (Deuteronomy 6:5; Leviticus 19:18). Jesus himself championed this simple yet profound message when he was asked which command was the most important:

Jesus replied, "You must love the LORD your God with all your heart, all your soul, and all your mind." This is the first and greatest commandment. A second is equally important: "Love your neighbor as yourself" (Matthew 22:37-39).

In alignment with the teaching of Moses and all prophets, our Rabbi championed a life of love for God, oneself, and one's neighbor.

A perusal of the newspaper or a glance at the television screen quickly reveals a world desperately in need of this simple, yet profound message. Followers of Jesus have been given this assignment to reflect God's love to the world. When he told us to love our neighbors, Jesus meant all of our neighbors, regardless of age, status, education, or any other potentially divisive issue. Once again, Mr. Rogers can help us here. I am convinced that our neighbors are craving the community that followers of Christ can provide. I am convinced that our lost, hurting, broken neighbors share the same feelings expressed in the last line of Mr. Rogers' theme song: *"Please won't you be my neighbor?"* [3]

Often this cry is disguised as addiction. Sometimes it masquerades as violence and hatred. But, in the deep recesses of their souls, our neighbors cry to simply be loved. As followers of Jesus, we are called to hear their cries and be their neighbors.

AUGUST 2018

CHAPTER ONE
Stepping into the Neighborhood

The Word became flesh and blood,
and moved into the neighborhood.
We saw the glory with our own eyes,
the one-of-a-kind glory,
like Father, like Son,
Generous inside and out,
true from start to finish.
John 1:14 (MSG)

The modern calendar we typically use to mark time is known as the Gregorian calendar. It begins in January and ends in December. This can be a bit confusing when we think about the placement of our Christian holidays because on a January to December calendar, Easter, the celebration of Jesus' resurrection, comes before Christmas, the celebration of Jesus' birth. For followers of Jesus, ending the year with the beginning of Jesus' story feels wrong on so many levels.

In contrast, the Christian calendar is arranged differently from the Gregorian calendar. It begins the year with the first Sunday of Advent and anticipation about the birth of Jesus and ends the year victoriously with Christ the King Sunday. The Christian calendar flows from Advent and Christmas into Ordinary Time and then on to Lent and Easter. Easter is followed by Pentecost which leads into an extended period of Ordinary Time until the end of the year.

The Christian calendar reflects the narrative found in the Bible that first anticipates the Messiah's birth, then celebrates his birth. The biblical epic continues as we remember the ministry, death, burial, resurrection, and ascension of Jesus and culminates with the gift of the Holy Spirit for all people as we join Jesus in his mission to the world.

This clash between our modern Gregorian calendar and the Christian calendar can create a kind of theological confusion. For followers of Jesus, our calendar confusion can wrongly lead us to put the atoning work of Jesus, which we focus on during Lent and Easter, before the incarnating work of Jesus, which is at the center of Advent and Christmas.

It's a matter of putting first things first. Stephen Covey calls "put first things first" one of the seven habits of highly effective people.[4] Highly effective followers of Jesus model their lives after Jesus' life. We seek to live into "the unforced rhythms of grace" (Matthew 11:28-30, MSG). Two out of the four Gospels begin with the Christmas story and the birth of Jesus. (Mark, the shorter Gospel excludes the birth narrative. John describes Jesus' birth theologically. Matthew and Luke give their own version of the birth narrative.) Such consistency forces us to ask: What does the birth of Jesus teach followers of Jesus? Why is putting the Christmas story first so essential?

There are many reasons, but let me suggest that the first and most important reason is the influence of Jesus' Incarnation on his followers and the world. The word *incarnation* does not appear in our English translations of the Bible. Instead, it comes from a Latin word that means "in the flesh." It's a word used by followers of Jesus to communicate the long-shared belief that Jesus was born fully human while also mysteriously remaining fully divine.

The Gospel of Luke describes this mystery as he tells the story of Mary's pregnancy. When Gabriel, God's angel, announces that Mary has been chosen to bear in her body the Messiah, Mary is puzzled because she is a virgin. "But how can this happen? I am a virgin" (Luke 1:34), the teenager asks. Here is how Gabriel responded: "The Holy Spirit will come upon you, and the power of the Most High will overshadow you. So the baby to be born will be holy, and he will be called the Son of God" (Luke 1:35). Divinity and humanity would mysteriously and supernaturally meet in the womb of this peasant girl.

Whether we think about it or not, we often announce our belief in the Incarnation of Jesus when we gather for weekly worship. In The Nicene Creed,[5] we declare:

We believe in one Lord, Jesus Christ,
the only Son of God,
eternally begotten of the Father,
God from God, Light from Light,
true God from true God,
begotten, not made,
of one Being with the Father;
through him all things were made.

These words boldly assert the full divinity of Jesus. Then in faith, followers of Jesus proclaim this about the full humanity of Jesus:

For us and for our salvation
  he came down from heaven,
  was incarnate of the Holy Spirit and the Virgin Mary
  and became truly human.

This is our mysterious yet sure belief as followers of Jesus. We follow One who was fully human and fully divine. That Jesus was both fully human and fully divine gives meaning not only to his birth but also to his ministry, death, and resurrection. The Incarnation of Jesus also profoundly shapes the life and ministry of those of us who follow the One born to Mary and Joseph in Bethlehem. In fact, the Incarnation of Jesus is massively important to the everyday life of Christians. Let me try and explain.

JESUS' NEIGHBORHOOD

I have served in my current church assignment, Grace Church in Cape Coral, Florida, for more than twenty-three years. Throughout more than two decades of working there, I have had lots of strange experiences. Right at the top of the list is something that happened early one morning many years ago. On the morning in question, I answered my phone and found myself speaking to Jeff, a member of our church and the station manager at the local Christian radio station.

"Jorge, have you seen the church sign this morning?"

"Jeff," I responded, "It's 6:00 a.m. No! I haven't seen the sign!"

"Well, go check it out right now and call me back," Jeff said—and with that he hung up.

I jumped in my car as the Florida sun was rising in the east and drove the mile and a half from my home to the church. When I pulled up, I was shocked. Someone had rearranged the letters on our well-lit sign. Instead of "Holy Discontent," the sermon title for that week, the sign read, "Holy S***."

Yup, that word. The word for "excrement." The word my mother would have washed out of my mouth with soap if I had said it in her presence. I took a picture for posterity's sake and quickly changed the sign before anymore of the thousands of people who drive by our church everyday saw it. When I called Jeff back, all he could do was howl in laughter.

Upon reflection, I almost wish I hadn't changed the sign so quickly. Yes, it was crass. Yes, it had a cuss word on it, but it's not a bad description of the mission given to followers of Jesus in this world. Hear me out on this. Just think about it—it's a pretty good summary of what followers of Jesus believe about the mystery of the Incarnation.

John, one of Jesus' disciples and the one who confidently called himself, "the disciple whom Jesus loved," wrote in his beautifully poetic introduction to his retelling of Jesus' life this description of the Incarnation: "And the Word became flesh and lived among us, and we have seen his glory, the glory as of a father's only son, full of grace and truth" (John 1:14, NRSV).

When God wanted to share God's love with this planet, John tells us that God sent Jesus to come and live with us. In the Greek, the word translated "lived among us" literally means "to fix one's tabernacle" or "to pitch a tent." God became flesh and pitched a tent with us.

Years ago, I heard a story that illustrates what it means for God to become one of us. There was a country boy who loved ants. He even had a favorite ant pile near the front of the house on his father's farm. One day he heard his father's tractor running. He looked outside and saw that his father was tilling the land close to his favorite ant pile. The boy ran as fast as he could toward the pile and began to scream at the top of his lungs: "Get down ants! Don't you know that my father's tractor will destroy your home?" But the ants kept on doing what ants do, collecting bits of food and busily building their ant pile. The boy frantically racked his brain to think of a way to save the ants. How could he communicate his concern to them? The answer struck like a lightning bolt: the only way to communicate with the ants was to become an ant!

When God wants to communicate with us, when God wants to show us what it means to be full of love and grace, when God wants us to know about God's concern and compassion for us, that's when God sends Jesus to become a human, to become one of us.

Eugene Peterson translated the beginning of John's poetry as: "The Word became flesh and blood, and moved into the neighborhood" (John 1:14, MSG). God, in Christ, stepped into our world. Jesus moved into our neighborhood. Heaven crashed into earth. Holiness became human and was laid to rest in the hay. Majesty in a manger. Divinity in diapers. Pick your alliteration of choice; the gist is that Jesus, the Word of God, became "flesh and blood." He became one of us. He moved into our zip code.

And into what kind of neighborhood was Jesus born? Like Jesus himself, this neighborhood was a mixed bag. There were good things to be sure—the beauty of creation, the love of family and friends, the warmth of community. But there were also bad things—the ugly brutality of an oppressive government and the frustrating hollowness of lifeless religion. The neighborhood into which Jesus was born was in desperate need of redemption. Much like our neighborhoods today, it was "holy s***."

If there had been real-estate apps and websites back then that rated neighborhoods the way we do now, Jesus' neighborhood would have received some pretty unfavorable ratings. How do we know this? Shortly after the beautiful poetry describing Jesus' divine and human nature in John, chapter 1, the same Gospel recounts the calling of Jesus' first apprentices. First, Jesus approached Peter, Andrew, and two other unnamed men. When he told them, "Come and follow me," they did. Then, the next day Jesus called Philip who in turn invited his friend Nathaniel to come and meet Jesus. Here's how John recalls this episode:

Philip went to look for Nathanael and told him, "We have found the very person Moses and the prophets wrote about! His name is Jesus, the son of Joseph from Nazareth." "Nazareth!" exclaimed Nathanael. "Can anything good come from Nazareth?" (John 1:45-46a).

From what scholars tell us, Nazareth was likely a small village of 150 or so people. Needless to say, it was not a hotbed of Jewish society. Because of its small size and relative insignificance, Nathaniel openly wondered about whether the Messiah could come from such a backwards place. This little Podunk hamlet, three days journey from Jerusalem, the great city of David, was surely too inconsequential to be the home of the Savior.

Regardless of the reason behind Nathaniel's harsh evaluation of Nazareth, it was a simple place. Jesus' neighborhood was not the center of political, religious, or commercial life. Our Savior was raised in an ordinary village by ordinary parents. Jesus took his place on planet Earth among the simplest so that all might find hope in him. Even the geography of Jesus' life was full of grace.

TEACH US TO PRAY

Around the age of thirty, Jesus left Nazareth and began to travel around the region teaching, preaching, and healing others. One day the apprentices of Jesus, who we typically call disciples, asked him a question: "Teacher, how do we pray?" It's a pretty good question, and it's exactly the type of question a student should ask a teacher. In response, Jesus, their rabbi, led them in what we call the Lord's Prayer.

The prayer begins with an acknowledgment that we are praying *to* someone. Jesus tells us that we can call God "our Father." The Hebrew word used here is *abba*, a very intimate term. That intimacy came fully alive for me on a trip I made to the Holy Land. My wife and I were in a museum gift shop in Jerusalem when a little boy cried out, "Abba! Abba!" He had become separated from his Dad and, as I looked at his face with tears streaming down his cheeks, he broke into a smile as he finally spotted his *abba* and ran into his arms. Jesus tells us that when we pray we are talking to our good and kind Father. This is an intimate relationship between us and our Abba.

But Jesus also taught us that Abba is lofty and holy and that God is in heaven. God is powerful and mighty. This is an important contrast. The same God who is in an intimate relationship with us also deserves our praise and devotion.

Jesus continues addressing God saying, "Hallowed be thy name." Our response to God needs to be like Isaiah who in the year that King Uzziah died, saw the Lord with his majestic robe filling the temple and served by angelic beings. Isaiah heard this declaration of God's character: "Holy, holy, holy is the LORD of Heaven's Armies! The whole earth is filled with his glory!" (Isaiah 6:b).

Isaiah experienced the only characteristic of God that the Bible records in triplicate. It's the same description that John records from his vision on the island of Patmos, "Holy, holy, holy" (Revelation 4:8). Isaiah is undone by this heavenly God and God's overwhelming holiness. All he can do is respond in praise, confession, and repentance.

I love the story told in C. S. Lewis' fantasy novel *The Lion, the Witch and the Wardrobe.* The book tells the story of four children who discover the magical kingdom of Narnia. The story is fun, but it's also a Christian allegory with Jesus represented by the lion Aslan. When in Narnia, the children meet Mr. and Mrs. Beaver, who describe the mighty lion to them. Lucy is worried about meeting a lion and asks if Aslan is safe, to which Mr. Beaver responds:

"Safe?" said Mr. Beaver; "don't you hear what Mrs. Beaver tells you? Who said anything about safe? 'Course he isn't safe. But he's good. He's the King, I tell you." [6] Like Aslan, God is good, but God is also holy, and holy isn't the same as safe.

Recently, a friend mentioned a potential ministry opportunity for him. He told me he was praying about it, but that he was inclined to say no. Then he added, "Jesus scares me too much not to at least pray about it." My friend was echoing Isaiah's experience of the holiness of God, and Jesus' prayer prompts his disciples to also address God as the heavenly Father who is worthy of praise, worship, and adoration.

From this point, Jesus' example prayer in Matthew 6:10-13 continues by laying out a series of four prayer requests. These requests include asking for God's daily provision ("give us this day our daily bread"), requesting forgiveness of sins and the capacity to forgive others ("forgives us our debts as we forgive our debtors"), and protection from temptation and the devil ("and lead us not into temptation, but deliver us from evil"). But Jesus' first request of God in this model prayer is: "May your Kingdom come soon. May your will be done on earth, as it is in heaven" (Matthew 6:10).

The first petition Jesus teaches us to include in our prayers is a request that God make this blue-green planet look like heaven. Jesus teaches us that first and foremost we should ask our good and great Father to do God's work in our world. Jesus could have taught his disciples to pray about any number of things, but he chose these four things and at the top of the list was a call for the kingdom of God to come to earth.

How do we see God's kingdom come to earth? How do we see God's will done here as it is in heaven? Through you and me! We are the answer to Jesus' prayer in this verse. Ordinary followers of Jesus are charged with working alongside God to make earth look like heaven. In a world full of vitriol and division, we get to be champions of peace and unity. In a world of hate, we get to be givers of love. For this to happen, we all have to learn to reflect the One who moved into our neighborhood. We have to become women and men who practice what we will refer to in this book as "neighboring."

You see, I could have left that crass message up on our church sign, because when followers of Jesus get it right, we, like Jesus, do holy work in an unholy place. We are called to do our work at the intersection between the saintly and the sinful, and it requires dogged determination. In this way, Jesus' Incarnation serves as a metaphor for his followers. Jesus stepped into our broken world, and we are not only invited but also are charged by God to step into the brokenness of our communities. We are in the "holy s***" business. This is what it means for us to love our neighbors. I don't just acknowledge this call theologically, I know it personally because I remember that someone loved me enough to step into the mess that was my life forty years ago.

MY STORY

I was born in February of 1960 in Santurce, Puerto Rico, as the second and middle child of Carmen and Hector Acevedo. I have an amazing older brother also named Hector and a spectacular younger sister named Sylvia. Following the end of World War II, as a young man my dad enlisted in what was then called the Army Air Corp and later became the United States Air Force. The oldest of six children, my dad had been raised on a simple farm in the country. My mom was a school teacher and the youngest of twelve children who were raised in the city center of a medium-sized town in Puerto Rico.

Puerto Ricans love to party and some of my earliest memories are of parties with my family. I remember Christmas at my grandfather's house in the country, complete with a roasted pig on an open fire, loud Latino music, fierce and sometimes argumentative conversations, and lots of booze. My first memories of drinking are from these family gatherings where I would sip from the leftovers that were left sitting around. I loved the taste of rum, coke, and lime mixed together. When you add to this experience the military

life on air bases and access to cheap liquor at the air-
man's club, you have the beginnings of a perfect storm
for alcohol abuse. As a child, I thought everyone drank
like the adults drank in our home. For us, this was our
family normal.

My first experience being drunk happened when
I was twelve years old. It was my brother's wedding
and they were serving pink champagne. I remember
sitting in the corner drinking the champagne like
it was water. The bubbles tickled my nose and my
stomach until eventually it quit tickling and started
making me sick. On the ride home from the reception, I hung my head out the car window and threw
up the whole way. For the next several days I was
sick, but I remember still really liking the feeling I had
from drinking. It was around this time that I discovered marijuana and realized I also really liked the
feeling I had when I smoked pot.

From the ages of twelve to seventeen, my interest
in drugs and alcohol increased. My story wasn't one of
immediate addiction or abuse; it was more situational.
When life was OK, I didn't use as much, but when life
became harder, I would use to excess. The more difficult my adolescent life, the more dependent I became
on substances.

I had two saving graces. First, because my mom
was a teacher, education was valued in our home and
expectations for good grades and regular studying
were ingrained in me early on. The second was my
love of sports. I was a decent athlete and sports eventually became my identity. The jersey and the letter
jacket gave my life meaning.

In 1975, I was a sophomore at Oak Ridge High
School in Orlando, Florida. I was playing on the junior

varsity football squad and was badly injured in the second game of the season. While I was running down the field on the opening kickoff, a huge guy hit me with a crack-back block and I shredded my right knee. Because my identity was so interlaced with sports, I played six more games with torn cartilage. The team doctor finally spotted my swollen knee and made me schedule an appointment with an orthopedic surgeon. My knee surgery kept me in the hospital for a week, on crutches for months, and in rehab for a year. The doctor told me I could no longer play sports, because the risk was just too high. Losing this identity as a jock sent me into a tailspin.

My junior year of high school was a blur. If I wasn't on the team, who was I? Like so many adolescents then and now, my identity was completely tied to others' perceptions of me. So I decided if I couldn't wear a jersey then I would be the life of the party. It was the height of the disco era. Remember *Saturday Night Fever*, John Travolta, and leisure suits? That became my new life.

A few years earlier Walt Disney World had opened and along with it came lots of nightclubs. My best friend Dennis and I lived this disco life in Orlando. The drinking age in Florida was 18, and Dennis had two cars: a van and a Datsun 280Z. We were a mobile party machine! Over time Friday and Saturday nights at the club turned into Wednesday nights at Nickle's Alley for nickel beer night. Skipping school and heading to the beach was a way of life—just our friends, our weed, and our kegs. Life was one big party.

By my senior year, I cared only about the next party, the next girl, and the next high. I kept up my grades and, in my mom's naïve way of thinking, as long as my grades were good I was good.

I was not good. I was halfway through my senior year, and I still had not taken my SATs for college. I really didn't care about my future. I had no purpose in life. I didn't care about going to college. I cared only about the next party.

It was at this point that God brought John into my life. John was the area director of Campus Crusade for Christ. Along with his team and his wife Karen, he would visit the campus of Oak Ridge High School looking for students with leadership potential. They believed if they could reach the school's teen leaders, then those leaders would reach their friends.

They found me right away. I was a leader of sorts; it's just that I was leading other students to join the party scene. John invited me to attend some of their meetings and I went. I won't credit myself with any spiritual insight at this point. I went because some of the cutest girls in our school were going. John and his team met at a community center. They engaged us in silly but fun games, played music off the radio, and ended every gathering with a short talk that eventually found its way to Jesus.

Slowly, throughout my senior year, I became more interested in what John had to say. I was drawn to his quirky humor, and I couldn't get my head around why an adult would care about a high school kid like me. I wasn't very interested in John's Jesus yet, but I was very interested in John. Later, John invited me and a handful of my friends to join a small group where we used a little three-ring binder called a "Discovery Book." The book asked questions like, "Who was Jesus?" and "What is the Bible about?"

One night in January of 1978, our group was meeting in my parents' living room. That night John said something like, "Jesus can give you a purpose and a meaning in life." In that moment, I asked the first serious question I had ever asked in our meetings: "John, really, what difference can Jesus make in my life?"

John replied, "Jorge, Jesus can give you a purpose and meaning for living your life. He's done it for me."

Notice that John didn't go down the "Jesus died for your sins" trail, because frankly, at the time, I didn't care about that. My life was fine in my mind, but I was desperate for purpose and meaning. For whatever reason, John's words made sense and touched a deep place in my soul. That night I knelt on the gold shag carpet in my living room (gold shag carpet was very cool in 1978), and I prayed to receive Christ. I asked Jesus to come into my life and I did what Sam Shoemaker said every human being can do: I gave as much of myself as I could to as much of God as I understood at the time.[7]

It was my starting point. To be completely honest, after John left that night, my buddies and I went out and got high to celebrate that I had become a Christian! Remember, I knew very little about God. Still, I can't explain it, but something happened inside me that night and in the following days. Words are limited when explaining the work of the Holy Spirit, but I knew that even though my lifestyle hadn't changed, God was with me. I didn't attend a church or read a Bible for the next six months, but I could feel something shifting inside me. It was mysterious and powerful.

Right after graduation John invited me to attend a Campus Crusade for Christ summer high school conference in Colorado. My parents, who were not yet followers of Jesus, not only bought me my first Bible but also paid for the conference as a graduation gift. It was in those mountains of Colorado that my discipleship truly began to take root. I learned that I could grow as a Christian by spending time with other Christ-followers, by reading the Bible and praying, and by serving others and sharing my faith. I learned what it meant to be an apprentice of Jesus, and I began the lifelong journey of what I now know is called "sanctification."

In June of 1978, I walked into Pine Castle United Methodist Church and I was home. I discovered a family to love me, mentors to walk with me, and a calling to serve God in full-time ministry. It was from this charismatic congregation that I learned how to worship our great God. They nurtured my spiritual gifts and released me to use them in their fellowship and our community. They backed it up with their financial support and helped pay for both my college and seminary education using church scholarship funds. But it all started when John incarnated Jesus for me at Oak Ridge High School. It began when John stepped into my mess and became my neighbor.

More than forty years later, I still ponder the reality that it was a parachurch ministry that reached me and not a local church. I did not walk down an aisle, surrender my life to Jesus, and take vows of membership at a local church under the guidance of an ordained pastor. Instead, I came to faith in Jesus in a community center and in my living room under the care of a kind Jesus-follower with no ecclesiastical pedigree, but instead had the courage and conviction to step into my neighborhood. John became a "go-to," neighboring Christ-follower rather than a "come-to" one.

BECOMING A "GO-TO" FOLLOWER OF JESUS

The apostle Paul was the ultimate go-to follower of Jesus. After his conversion on the road to Damascus, Paul had a conversation with Jesus in a vision where Jesus commissioned him, "Go, for I will send you far away to the Gentiles!" (Acts 22:21).

Paul obeyed this charge and undertook three extended journeys to establish missionary outposts of the Kingdom throughout Asia Minor. Paul gives us a peek into his go-to heart in 1 Thessalonians 2:7-12. As usual, Paul's letters were a mixture of encouragement and correction. In these six verses, he models four characteristics of a neighboring follower of Jesus.

1. "Go-to" Followers of Jesus Are Gentle

Here's how Paul begins: "As apostles of Christ we certainly had a right to make some demands of you, but instead we were like children among you. Or we were like a mother feeding and caring for her own children" (1 Thessalonians 2:7).

Paul was an authority to his followers. He was the missionary who came to Thessalonica and established the church there (Acts 17:1-9). He could have leaned into this authority, but that is not what this neighboring missionary did. Instead, Paul uses two different images in this passage to describe his approach to the people of Thessalonica: a child and a nursing mother. Together, these images tell us that Paul coupled humility with relentless tenderness and patience.

Let's think about these images for a moment. In the first century, children were regarded as property and had no rights. Paul, Silas, and Timothy reminded the church they could have been demanding, but that was not the approach these Christ-followers chose. Instead, Paul and his coworkers were humble. They were childlike.

The image of a mother feeding and caring for her children is then combined with this humility. In my mind's eye, this image brings back memories of my wife Cheryl after the birth of our two sons, Daniel and Nathan. I marveled at the patience she displayed teaching both boys to nurse. It took time and patience to teach these newborn babies how to eat. This powerful image of a nursing mother describes the character of Paul's way with the community.

There's a bumper sticker I love that says, "Please be patient with me, 'cause God ain't finished with me yet." I like that, and I believe it's true even in the lives of people who are far from God. We believe in the prevenient grace of God; that's what we call the grace that God gives to us even before we know God's love. God is at work long before we discover God's presence in our lives. God is patient and that means we can be, too. God has certainly been patient with me and so have other followers of Christ.

Forty years later, I think back and it still amazes me that John and his team reached out to high school students like us. They had to know that when they left our lunch tables we made fun of them. Nevertheless, they were gentle with us. They were relentlessly tender and patient. For me, one of the gifts of social media has been the ability to catch up with many of my high school classmates. There are dozens upon dozens of them who today are followers of Jesus and serving God in the world and in the church because of John and his neighboring team.

One of the most beautiful examples of God's grace at Grace Church is Rochelle. Today, she is on staff at the Central campus of Grace Church and leads the recovery ministry that ministers to more than five hundred people in recovery every week! Sadly, Rochelle's story is not an uncommon one. She grew up in a home with divorced parents, lived in foster homes and with other family members, and was a victim of physical and sexual abuse. At the age of twenty-three, she found herself addicted to drugs and with three little boys to raise by herself. In her testimony, Rochelle talks about her personal encounter with gentle, neighboring followers of Jesus:

> For over six years, I tried to get sober, going to Alcoholics Anonymous, Cocaine Anonymous, and Celebrate Recovery. I wanted to be sober so bad. I would come into Celebrate Recovery at Grace Church and cry and cry through worship and, by the time the lesson was half way through, I would be gone to the dope man and then pick up my kids afterwards.

> I will always be grateful for the hope that was being given to my children in Grace Place (our children's ministry). You see, while I was a mess, God was working in my kids' lives. I'll never forget one night in a drunken rage, I was trying to run over my kids' father with a truck. Evan, my son, said to me, "Mom, God has a plan and a purpose for us and it is going to be OK."

> I was trying to get sober. I was attending the Central campus and showing up there to volunteer to try and keep myself busy. In February of 2011, I was "dragged" to my baptism. I chose not to go that morning because I got high the night before and didn't feel worthy. Yet Pastor Arlene made my friend Sharon come get me

and she dragged me and the kids to church anyway. They reminded me that even when I turn my back on God, God does not turn his back on me.

Within two months, I had lost everything. I had cut off all contact with everyone I knew and loved and had no idea where my kids were. I was on the run and on Lee County's Most Wanted List for jumping bail. I was smoking crack and hiding in suitcases from the drug man. I dug myself into a hole so bad. I had absolutely nothing left. It got so bad that when I tried to get high to numb the pain, it wouldn't work anymore. I now know God allowed me to get in a place where there was no way out but through God.

On August 12, 2011, I literally gave up. I had no more fight in me. I was so broken and so lost. I turned myself into the bounty hunters. I knew I had to change, and something had to give. It was in jail where, for the first time in my life, I realized the true meaning of powerlessness and that my life was completely unmanageable. My plea offer was five years in prison, and I was told that if I went to trial it could be more.

I began working the steps of recovery in jail and reading the Bible a lot. I spent every day seeking God's truth. The more I read, the more I prayed, and the more happiness and calmness came over me. It was in those moments I realized the grace that God had been showing me all these years here through the people at

*Grace Church. I wasn't sure who this person
was I was becoming or where it was going to
end up. Second Corinthians 5:17 says, "Anyone
who belongs to Christ has become a new person. The old life is gone; a new life has begun!"
Without a shadow of doubt, I realized that the
old me no longer lived.*

Rochelle often says to our Grace Church people:
"You kept coming back again and again. No matter
what I did, you kept coming back." This is the kind
of humility coupled with relentless tenderness and
patience that neighboring followers of Jesus display.

2. "Go-to" Followers of Jesus Are Relational

In 1978 when I finally surrendered to Jesus' love,
I kept hearing people in my new church talk about
their "life verse." I was such a new Christian that I
didn't know Malachi from Matthew when it came to
the Bible, but the idea intrigued me. At the same time,
I didn't want to just choose a verse at random, so I
decided I would wait and let my life verse come to me.

Two years after my conversion, I felt called into
ministry. My pastor encouraged me to attend Asbury
College so, in August of 1980, without my parents'
blessing, I sold my 1976 candy-apple-red Chevy
Camaro (it had a 350, four-barrel engine with a 250-
watt cassette player and two 6-by-9 coaxial speakers
in the back—just a little more therapy and I'll be over
selling it) and headed off to Wilmore, Kentucky, to prepare for my future as a pastor. I thought that if I was
going to be a minister, I probably needed to know the
Bible, so I became a Bible major. It was in those early
days at Asbury College when my life verse came to
me: "We loved you so much that we shared with you

not only God's Good News but our own lives, too"
(1 Thessalonians 2:8).

Over the years, I've noticed a few things about
what Paul says in this verse. First, Paul genuinely
loved the followers of Jesus in Thessalonica. He uses
a form of the word *agape* here. This word is used for
the kind of unconditional, relentless love that God
has for us and that Jesus invites his followers to have
for others. It's also interesting to note that this love
is expressed to the people in Thessalonica by Paul
preaching the good news of Jesus to them and enter-
ing into a genuine relationship with them. Paul gave
them both Jesus and his heart. It's hard to be a neighboring follower of Jesus without relationally investing
in people. Paul had relational "skin in the game."

You know, if God only wanted us to have information, God could have just dropped a book to earth or
made a YouTube video. If God only wanted to give us
physical healing, God could have just sent us medicine. If God only wanted to bring justice, God could
have made that happen too. But God wanted something more—God wanted a relationship with us. That's
why God sent Jesus to earth.

Loving our neighbors is mostly a ministry of
presence. Proclaiming the good news flows from
being present with our neighbors, from being Jesus-
followers who go to others instead of waiting for them
to come to us. This is what Paul and his teammates
did in Thessalonica in the first century and what we, in
the twenty-first century, are invited to do in our neighborhoods today. Loving our neighbors is not an arms-
length transaction; it requires sharing life together.

Bill Hinson once served as Senior Pastor of First
United Methodist Church in Houston, Texas. Under

Bill's leadership this congregation had become the largest United Methodist Church in America with over fourteen thousand members. But Bill started his ministry in much humbler circumstances at a small rural church in South Georgia. I remember him telling a story in a sermon about trying to reach one of his neighbors for Christ. Week after week Bill would invite the man to church with no success. Eventually, Bill learned that the man was the finest frog-gigger in the county, so one afternoon Bill asked him, "Do you know where I can get me a mess of frog legs?"

The man's face lit up and he said, "Why I go frog-gigging every Friday night and I'll be glad to take you along."

That Friday night and every following Friday night for a long time, Bill Hinson and his neighbor buddy gigged for frogs. One Sunday morning Bill looked up and saw his gigging partner sitting on the back row. A few Sundays later when Bill invited people to follow Jesus, the man stepped out of his seat and came forward. Bill concluded, "That man had been frog-gigged into the church!" There's an old saying that goes, "Make a friend. Be a friend. Lead a friend to Christ." It's what neighboring followers of Jesus do.

The church and community I serve in southwest Florida is a growing and diverse community. One of the groups in our community that was being forgotten was the special-needs community, and Grace Church sensed a calling from God to serve them. First, we started a buddy ministry for special-needs children and students who attended our weekend worship services. This allowed the parents or guardians of special-needs children to attend worship, while having the assurance that their precious loved ones were being cared for and engaged in ministry. This weekly ministry inspired a respite night outreach for the special-needs community. This event allowed parents or guardians to leave their loved ones and other family members with us at the church for a three-hour respite to do anything the caregivers wanted to do. As wonderful as these ministries are, they were primarily come-to not go-to ministries.

In a way that only God could orchestrate, a group of leaders in our church got a nudge from the Holy Spirit to begin a ministry for people with special needs who had aged out of the county school system. In Florida the state will educate a child with special needs until he or she is twenty-two. After that age, there are very few options for adults with special needs. This group of leaders dreamed of launching a place where adults with special needs could partner with mentors to develop business models and create products that would be sold on the open market. That's how Exceptional Entrepreneurs was birthed (_www.egracechurch.com/ee/_).

Today this ministry has a full-time director and a handful of part-time staff, along with a cadre of neighboring followers of Jesus who reflect Jesus to both the adults with special needs in our community and their families. Together, they are researching, developing, and producing everything from yard art and Adirondack chairs to honey sticks and wall art. These creations are then sold to the wider local community in a stand-alone store. Exceptional Entrepreneurs has become a unique missional community, but more importantly it's become a vessel for life transformation for all those who are involved in its ministry.

A few years after its start-up, one of the volunteers who was not a believer was led to Christ by one of our staff. She attended our membership class, was baptized, and joined Grace Church. Several of her friends with special needs attended her baptism. Afterwards, they asked Heather about her baptism and four of them asked to be baptized as well.

I'll never forget when the program director called me to ask about the procedure for all of this. I explained that in our church baptism is connected to membership and that I would need to meet with the participants who had asked to be baptized and with their families. Two were living with parents and two sisters were living independently. I met with them in what had to be the strangest but most beautiful new member class ever. These four amazing people just "got it." They had Jesus living in their heart, and they wanted to be baptized.

We made plans for them to be baptized at our weekend services. On that day we showed a testimony video about the ministry and their story and then I baptized them. On our way home that Sunday afternoon, I told my wife Cheryl, who has spent more than twenty years serving students with special needs and their families in the public-school system: "I can die today. Ministry will never get better than this!"

It all began with a rag-tag group of neighboring followers of Jesus taking Jesus at his word and loving both God and neighbors as they loved themselves. This is what it means to give our neighbors "not only God's good news but our own lives, too."

3. "Go-to" Followers of Jesus Are Authentic

As Paul continues his message to the followers of Jesus in Thessalonica, he reminds them of his integrity and that of his fellow missionaries. Paul writes: "You yourselves are our witnesses—and so is God—that we were devout and honest and faultless toward all of you believers" (1 Thessalonians 2:10). Paul reminds the people in Thessalonica that there is an alignment between the message of Christ-followers and the lives they live. This is true authenticity.

People who are far from God are looking for women and men who are the genuine article. I'm not suggesting some kind of unhealthy perfectionism or rigid fanaticism. Being faultless does not mean being flawless. Instead, I'm saying that it's important to remember that people who follow Jesus have not only been freed from the penalty of sin but also from the power of sin. One of our greatest witnesses to this encounter with Jesus is a transformed life.

Augustine was the life of the party before becoming a Christian. One day after becoming a Christian, he was walking in front of one of his favorite old hangouts—a bar. He looked up and walking towards him on the street was a prostitute he had known in his previous life. Smiling, she assumed that Augustine was over his little religious phase and had returned to where he truly belonged. As they approached each other, he continued to look ahead and passed by without even acknowledging her.

"Augustine, don't you recognize me?" she asked.

He stopped, turned, looked at her, and said, "Yes, I recognize you, but it is no longer me."

When we become Christians, new creations in Christ, it is no longer us. We are different. Our lives are different.

Within our Grace Church community, the ministry where I've seen this kind of authenticity lived out best is the recovery ministry. For the past eighteen years, we have engaged in recovery ministry at Grace Church using Saddleback's "Celebrate Recovery" model (*www.celebraterecovery.com*). Every Friday, 250 to 300 adults and children gather at our Cape Coral campus for dinner, a large-group worship gathering, and either issue-specific or gender-specific small groups (*www.egracechurch.com/cr/*). Celebrate Recovery is not a worship service. Instead it's a weekly, community-based, recovery experience. We've recently rebranded the ministry as "Choose Recovery."

When a person shows up at church on a Friday night, they are usually pretty desperate for a life change. We use the time to talk about our addictions and how they keep us from growing into the men and women God wants us to become. In the recovery community when a person is struggling, a seasoned member will ask: "Are you working the steps?" "Are you going to meetings?" and "Do you have a sponsor?" These three components give integrity to a person's journey of recovery and the answer is either "Yes" or "No." These recovery benchmarks give participants in the program authenticity in their personal recovery.

In 1872, John Wesley penned "The Character of a Methodist." This sermon outlines what Wesley believed were the attitudes and actions that gave integrity and authenticity to those who are a part of the Methodist movement. He writes:

> *"What then is the mark? Who is a Methodist, according to your own account?" I answer: A Methodist is one who has "the love of God shed abroad in his heart by the Holy Ghost given unto him"; one who "loves the Lord his God with all his heart, and with all his soul, and with all his*

*mind, and with all his strength. God is the joy of
his heart, and the desire of his soul; which is constantly crying out, "Whom have I in heaven but
thee? and there is none upon earth that I desire
beside thee! My God and my all! Thou art the
strength of my heart, and my portion for ever!"* [8]

For Wesley and his team, a Methodist was simply
one who had experienced the love and grace of God
through the power and presence of the Holy Spirit.
In the rest of his sermon, Wesley goes deeper on the
"marks" or "practices" of a Methodist. My old seminary
professor Dr. Steve Harper has said there are five: [9]

1. Love God
2. Rejoice in God
3. Give thanks
4. Pray constantly
5. Love others

These practices give Methodists authenticity. Much
like working the steps, going to meetings, and having
a sponsor give a person in recovery the tools to get
and stay free from compulsive behaviors, Methodists
believe these practices allow them to be witnesses to
a life that is "devout and honest and faultless."

4. "Go-to" Followers of Jesus Are Passionate

A little boy came home from church one Sunday
and his momma asked him about Sunday school. He
responded, "Momma, I met Jesus' grandma today!"

"You met Jesus' grandma?" she replied quizzically.
"How did you know you met Jesus' grandma?"

"Well," her son said, "all our teacher did was show
us pictures of Jesus and tell us stories about him. She's
gotta' be Jesus' grandma!"

What's your passion in life? Are you so passionate about Jesus that some sweet little boy might mistake you for Jesus' grandma? I don't mean this in a weird way, but I do think we should be passionate for Jesus and the things he was passionate about. We need to be at least as passionate as we are for our favorite sport teams or hobbies. We see the intensity of Paul and his team here:

> And you know that we treated each of you as a father treats his own children. We pleaded with you, encouraged you, and urged you to live your lives in a way that God would consider worthy. For he called you to share in his Kingdom and glory (1 Thessalonians 2:11-12).

Again, notice the relational imagery in these verses. Paul began with the metaphors of a child and a nursing mother in verse 7 and ends this section comparing his behavior to that of a father in verses 11–12. Fathers in the first century were not known for their kindness and consideration. In a patriarchal culture, dad was "large and in charge" and, frankly, could sometimes be cruel and abusive. Wives and children were often treated like slaves. Here, Paul reimagines what it means to be a father when he says that, like a father, he "pleaded," "encouraged," and "urged" Jesus' followers on their walk of faith. These are passionate words. We all know that passion is contagious. This passion for Jesus influences everything it touches with the gentle, relational, and authentic nature of Christ.

Years ago, I read the amazing story of Gregory Robertson, a 35-year-old Phoenix man, who performed a mid-air rescue of Debbie Williams. Debbie had jumped from a plane with five others. At 9000 feet she collided with one of the group members and was left unconscious, spinning helplessly towards the ground. Gregory Roberts had jumped out of the plane also, but was above the other jumpers. When he saw what happened, he pinned his arms and legs together and sped downwards at 180 mph towards Debbie. He finally caught up with her at 3,500 feet and released her chute just 10 seconds before she would have hit the ground. When he was interviewed later Gregory Williams said, "Somebody tried to die in my drop zone, and I didn't like it." [10] Mr. Williams understood that he had a responsibility to those in his drop zone. That's passion!

Around our church we use a phrase that describes the joy of watching Jesus transform a life: "I got a front-row seat at life change!" Throughout my twenty-three years at Grace Church, I have been privileged to see God change hundreds of lives. One of my favorite stories involves Harold and John. Harold came to Grace Church through our recovery ministry. He found God in the rooms of recovery and Jesus at Grace Church. With great passion, he would tell people about the transformation Jesus was making in his life.

This passion led Harold to befriend Cathy, John's wife. John's drug addiction was destroying his relationship with Cathy and their four children. Cathy invited her new friend Harold to pray for John. Harold put feet to those prayers as he neighbored John and struck up a friendship with him. One day, Harold gave John his business card and passionately and sincerely told him, "If you ever need me, you call me and I'll be there for you." That time would come sooner than either man expected.

One Saturday John found his bottom, as they say in recovery. He got "sick and tired of being sick and tired." As he drove to the church parking lot, he thought, *There are always people at that church so I'll find someone to talk to.* When John arrived, the parking lot was empty, but he remembered Harold's words, "If you ever need me, you call me and I'll be there for you." He called and Harold not only answered but also met John in the parking lot. It was there that a passionate, neighboring follower of Jesus helped John, a drug addict, open the door to God. John was marvelously and beautifully transformed by Jesus.

Neighboring Christ-followers are gentle, relational, authentic, and passionate, and it's how they live their lives as the body of Christ.

Questions for Personal Reflection and Group Discussion

1. What does the Incarnation mean to you? How does it affect your faith to know that Jesus "became flesh and blood and moved into the neighborhood"?

2. What does it mean to call God "holy"? How does God's holiness play a role in your faith? How do we reflect God's holiness to others in our community?

3. How did you first learn about God? Was there someone like John in your life? Who first embodied for you what it meant to be a follower of Jesus?

4. How can followers of Jesus share their lives with their neighbors? Tell about a time you shared your life with a neighbor or someone shared with you?

5. What are you passionate about? How can you put this passion to work as a follower of Christ?

CHAPTER TWO
Look, Listen, and Learn

Go to the people. Live with them. Learn from them. Love them.
Start with what they know. Build with what they have. —Lao Tzu

In the summer of 2013, I was on a four-month sabbatical. I had been honored with a sizable grant that allowed my wife Cheryl and me to spend two months tracing the life of Jesus in Israel, Paul in Italy, Greece, and Turkey, and the Wesleys in England, Scotland, Ireland, and Northern Ireland. On this particular day, Cheryl and I were in Northern Ireland in the small hamlet of Downpatrick, the burial city of the great Saint Patrick.

Upon arriving, we made our way to the St. Patrick Centre. The museum curator told us that our experience at the museum would be more meaningful if we first toured St. Patrick's Cathedral and visited the grave of St. Patrick in the churchyard. We exited the Centre, turned right, and made another immediate right to walk up a concrete path and ascend a hill to the Cathedral. As we began to make our short climb, we bumped into a group of tourists who were gathered around a marble inset in the sidewalk. It was covered with debris, and they were sweeping it off with their feet to read the inscription. Cheryl and I stepped around them and continued to make our climb.

When we arrived at the top of the small hill, we noticed another marble inset in the path, similar to the previous one. It also was covered with leaves, sticks, and dirt, so we began to sweep it off with our feet as well. Much to our delight, we read these words from John Wesley's journal dated June 10, 1785:

> *We came to Downpatrick where the preaching house being too small, we repaired, as usual to the Grove; a most lovely place, very near the most venerable ruins of the cathedral.*[11]

We looked around and to our astonishment, we were standing in the very grove where John Wesley preached! Now for a United Methodist preacher to happen upon the very site where John Wesley actually preached was like a child's first visit to Disney World. I was giddy. I said to Cheryl: "You go inside the Cathedral. I'm going to roll around in the grass and pray that the anointing of John Wesley falls upon me." It was a serendipitous gift of God.

After our sabbatical, I had time to reflect upon this generous gift from God and what it meant to come upon this Wesley plaque and the grove where he preached. I knew that most of the Methodist movement during John Wesley's life was headquartered in London and Bristol. For Cheryl and me to get to Downpatrick in Northern Ireland from England literally took us days by planes, trains, and automobiles. Yet, John Wesley had traveled the same journey on horseback and by foot with a band of missionaries. He did all of this without the advantages of our modern world. He didn't have a smartphone for directions or a tablet for entertainment and distraction. Instead, he wrote letters and pamphlets to communicate to the people called Methodists which would help shape a fresh expression of church. He worked together with these followers of Jesus to transform Great Britain on horseback!

By the time of John Wesley's death, there were nearly 115,000 people in the Methodist system of discipleship in the United Kingdom and the Americas! "An indication of his organizational genius, we know exactly how many followers Wesley had when he died: 294 preachers, 71,668 British members, 19 missionaries (5 in mission stations), and 43,265 American members with 198 preachers."[12] United Societies with class meetings and bands sprung up all over England, Scotland, and Wales and then jumped the Irish Sea to Ireland. Later, Thomas Coke and Francis Asbury would champion the Methodist movement in the United States.

JOHN WESLEY, THE METHODISTS, AND FIELD PREACHING

Think with me, for a moment, about the story of John Wesley. He was the son of an Anglican priest, and he followed in his father Samuel's footsteps to become an Anglican priest himself. To Wesley, proper form and decorum were essential to being an Oxford-trained priest in the Church of England. After a horrible ministry experience in Georgia, John Wesley returned home to England defeated yet searching for more of God. The witness of the Moravians, a German Christian community, coupled with the mentoring of Peter Boehler, drew Wesley closer to the experience of God's grace for which he hungered. On May 24, 1738, it happened. Wesley wrote in his journal of his encounter with God at Aldersgate Street:

> *In the evening, I went very unwillingly to*
> *a society in Aldersgate Street, where one was*
> *reading Luther's preface to the Epistle to the*
> *Romans. About a quarter before nine, while he*
> *was describing the change which God works in*
> *the heart through faith in Christ, I felt my heart*
> *strangely warmed. I felt I did trust in Christ,*
> *Christ alone, for salvation; and an assurance*
> *was given me that He had taken away my sins,*
> *even mine, and saved me from the law of sin*
> *and death.*[13]

John Wesley's life was forever altered at Aldersgate. From this moment on, with his warm heart and sharp mind, Wesley and his brother Charles led a renewal movement from within the Church of England. The mission of Jesus became the mission of the early Methodists.

Yet, the Anglican Church with all its rich history was predominately meant for Britain's elite. The working poor were marginalized and missing from the religious life of sixteenth-century Britain. This group soon became Wesley's "target audience." However, Wesley knew that the strategies of the Anglican church would not reach the poor. So, without changing the mission of Jesus to "go make disciples," Wesley changed strategies.

After Aldersgate, Wesley quickly realized that much of his training as an Anglican priest would not reach the people on the margins of British society. It didn't take long for Wesley and firebrand preaching to put him at odds with Anglican leadership, and he was summarily forbidden from preaching in their churches. Then, Wesley received an invitation from George Whitefield, the great evangelist, to come see, of all things, "field preaching." In the 1700s, this practice was considered uncouth and irreverent. Wesley writes in his journal from March 31, 1739:

> *In the evening I reached Bristol and met Mr. Whitefield there. I could scarcely reconcile myself at first to this strange way of preaching in the fields, of which he set me an example on Sunday; I had been all my life (till very lately) so tenacious of every point relating to decency and order that I should have thought the saving of souls almost a sin if it had not been done in a church.* [14]

This first brush with field preaching and George Whitefield challenged the finely-honed sensibilities of John Wesley. But then, just two days later, Mr. Wesley found himself embracing this new methodology. He notes in his journal:

> *At four in the afternoon, I submitted to be more vile and proclaimed in the highways the glad tidings of salvation, speaking from a little eminence in a ground adjoining to the city, to about three thousand people . . . .* [15]

This new strategy was a profound shift for Wesley and the early Methodists as they worked to reach people the Anglican church could not. This "vile" way would be the portal through which many new converts were made and became part of the Methodist discipleship system of United Societies, Class Meetings, and Bands.

STAY ON MISSION! CHANGE THE METHOD!

John Wesley, whether he was conscious of it or not, was simply following the lead of the great church planter Paul. Paul worked hard to harass and oppress early converts to Christianity before he was transformed by God's grace into a pillar of the early church. With the pedigree of a Roman father and a Jewish mother, Paul was called by the Holy Spirit to spread the movement of Jesus beyond its original Jewish audience.

His church planting method was pretty simple. He and his companions would arrive in a city and Paul would find the local synagogue. He would appeal to "all things Jewish" by engaging in spiritual conversations about the promised Messiah. Some would reject his message, some would be interested in more conversation, and some were converted to faith in Christ. Paul was constantly appealing to a kind of common ground between his Jewish and Gentile friends. He would stay in the city long enough to raise up a leadership team and set them apart before either leaving or getting run out of town by those who rejected his message. Then, Paul and his team would do it all over again in a new place. It was simple and it worked.

For example, in Acts 17, Luke records that Paul and his team were on their second missionary adventure. Acts 16 records their amazing ministry in Philippi. People from every social stratum became part of the body of Christ in Philippi. Luke documents three conversions in particular: Lydia, a wealthy businesswoman; a slave girl; and a Roman jailer who all were transformed by the gospel of Jesus. After leaving Philippi, Paul and his helpers make their way to Thessalonica. Luke records in Acts 17:2a, "As was Paul's custom, Paul went to the synagogue service . . . ."

Paul was obeying the commission Jesus had given the first followers of Jesus to go as Spirit-embolden witnesses from Jerusalem to Judea to Samaria and to the ends of the earth (see Acts 1:8). When Paul arrived in Thessalonica, there was no missionary outpost of the Kingdom in that region. Paul immediately put his missionary strategy to work and went to the synagogue. As often happened for Paul, some violently disagreed with his message. In Thessalonica, the good news of Jesus disrupted the community so much that the city leaders declared:

> "Paul and Silas have caused trouble all over the world," they shouted, "and now they are here disturbing our city, too. And Jason has welcomed them into his home. They are all guilty of treason against Caesar, for they profess allegiance to another king, named Jesus" (Acts 17:6a-7).

Then, as today, the gospel has a way of disrupting the lives of the comfortable. Quickly, the believers in Thessalonica rushed Paul and his team out of town to Berea, likely fearing for their safety. Luke records it this way: "That very night the believers sent Paul and Silas to Berea. When they arrived there, they went to the Jewish synagogue" (Acts 17:10).

Notice once again the strategy of this missionary band. They had just been hustled out of town for their own protection, yet once again, they went to the synagogue. We're told that their missionary work in Berea went very well. People were open, even eager, to learn from Paul. These were good days until some Jewish leaders from Thessalonica arrived in Berea and stirred up trouble. Once again, Paul and some of his team were forced to leave town. This time they made their way to the Greek city of Athens where Paul's mission would continue. However, this time we see that he changes up his method.

As they prepared to leave Berea and head to Athens, Paul left behind two important leaders: Silas and Timothy. Luke shares what Paul did while he waited for them to rejoin the team in Athens:

> *While Paul was waiting for them in Athens, he was deeply troubled by all the idols he saw everywhere in the city. He went to the synagogue to reason with the Jews and God-fearing Gentiles, and he spoke daily in the public square to all who happened to be there (Acts 17:16-17).*

In this passage, we see a significant shift in Paul's methodology of establishing new churches. He shifts from the synagogue to the marketplace. As I've wondered about the reasons for this change, two in particular come to mind. The first is simple and a bit more direct. Maybe Paul was simply tired of getting his head kicked in by religious and civil leaders in the cities he visited and decided to try a new method while hoping for a different result. Working with those in recovery I've often heard the familiar quote, "Insanity is trying the same thing over and over again expecting a different result." Maybe this is Paul's response to receiving such a negative response over and over.

Secondly, Paul may have realized that the Greek context demanded a different strategy. N.T. Wright explains that until Paul got to Athens, his major opponents in spreading the gospel were zealous Jews and the economic and political forces of mighty Rome.[16] Now Paul is in a culture where the prevailing worldview centered around ancient philosophies. Would the same way of presenting the good news to Jews and Romans work for the philosophical Greeks? A different culture would likely require a different approach.

Luke tells us that Paul was "deeply troubled" by the idols he saw. When I looked at this verse in the Greek, I found that it referred to Paul's *pneuma* or "spirit" being troubled, perplexed, stirred, or agitated. The question we're left to ask is, "Why?" Why was Paul's spirit so deeply affected by the idolatry of the Greeks? Was it simply a moral issue, or was it that his heart was broken at how lost they were? I have to believe it's the latter. Paul might have been angry, but I don't think his anger was directed at the people. He was what I like to call "good and mad" not "bad and mad." Paul was mad at how the Athenians had been led astray.

Think about Jesus' ministry. Repeatedly, our Rabbi saw the brokenness of people and it filled his heart with compassion. Matthew describes Jesus' compassion this way:

> *Jesus traveled through all the towns and villages of that area, teaching in the synagogues and announcing the Good News about the Kingdom. And he healed every kind of disease and illness. When he saw the crowds, he had compassion on them because they were confused and helpless, like sheep without a shepherd (Matthew 9:35-36).*

Jesus was moved in the deep recesses of his soul at the brokenness and confusion that he saw in people. In Athens, Paul had this same kind of deep-seated compassion stirring deep within his soul.

There's a song we sometimes sing at my church called "Hosanna" (recorded by the Hillsong Worship Team). The following words always bring tears to my eyes, "Break my heart for what breaks yours . . . Everything I am for your kingdom's cause."[17]

We see this brokenheartedness in Jesus as he walked the slopes of the Mount of Olives and made his way into Jerusalem:

*But as he (Jesus) came closer to Jerusalem
and saw the city ahead, he began to weep. "How
I wish today that you of all people would understand the way to peace. But now it is too late,
and peace is hidden from your eyes. Before long
your enemies will build ramparts against your
walls and encircle you and close in on you from
every side. They will crush you into the ground,
and your children with you. Your enemies will
not leave a single stone in place, because you
did not recognize it when God visited you" (Luke
19:41-44).*

Jesus was heartbroken over brokenness and lost-
ness. In these words, which many believe point to the
fall of Jerusalem in AD 70, Jesus shares with us that
beautiful blend of truth-telling and compassion. The
One who became flesh was indeed as John described
him, "full of grace and truth" (John 1:14, CEB). Jesus in
Jerusalem and Paul in Athens model how we can meld
a tender heart with a tough mind.

Father Henri Nouwen wrote the classic book *The
Wounded Healer* to help clergy understand this side of
Jesus. Though he directs his words to ministers, I believe
they apply to all followers of Jesus when he writes:

*"For the minister is called to recognize the
sufferings of his time in his own heart, and
make to that recognition the starting point of
his service. Whether he tries to enter into a dis-
located world, relate to a convulsive generation,
or speak to a dying person, his service will not
be perceived as authentic unless it comes from
a heart wounded by the suffering about which
he speaks."[18]*

I love the idea of suffering as the "starting point" of our mission. I think this was Paul's attitude as he walked the streets of Athens.

To listen to many Christ-followers today, you would think the world is "heading to hell in a handbasket." To be fair, much in our world today confirms such a judgment. From our treatment of the unborn and immigrants to our vitriol aimed at one another in our human family, there is much that indicates we've lost the best of our humanity. Callousness seems to reign in our culture. Yet, Paul models for us a better way forward. We do not need to throw up our hands in despair. Instead, we can find a common ground for conversation about the idolatry of our day. For Paul that meant a strategic shift in methodology from the synagogue to the marketplace.

WHERE IS THE PAIN IN YOUR CITY?

Years ago our church hosted an event for church leaders at the Florida Annual Conference of The United Methodist Church. We invited Al and Deb Hirsch, two remarkable thinkers and practitioners in the missional movement around the world. They are helping the church think in new, innovative, and Spirit-led ways about how to join Jesus in his mission. As part of her presentation, Deb said something that has stuck with me ever since: "The heartbeat of the city is where the pain is."[19]

My mouth dropped at the simple profundity of her evaluation. Almost everything in my pain-averted life leads me to run away from those places of pain. Yet, God is calling the Church of Jesus to be a neighbor to people who are far from God in these places. It's why John Wesley and the early Methodists focused on the poor of England.

Danielle Strickland is a Salvation Army officer who has led a number of ministries in helping establish justice and anti-trafficking initiatives throughout the world. In her book *A Beautiful Mess* she comments on these first words of the Bible: "In the beginning God created the heavens and the earth. The earth was formless and empty, and darkness covered the deep waters. And the Spirit of God was hovering over the surface of the waters" (Genesis 1:1-2).

Danielle's paraphrase of Genesis 1:1-2 reads like this: "God created the heavens and earth—all you see, all you don't see. Earth was a soup of nothingness, a bottomless emptiness, an inky blackness. God's Spirit brooded like a bird above the watery abyss." [20]

It's a beautiful and poetic rendering, and it reminds us that even in creation, God's Spirit hovers in those lifeless, dead places. Danielle goes on to comment, "The imagery is potent: of God above the chaos, yet strongly present in it." [21]

I suggest that like Jesus and Paul, followers of Jesus are invited to do God's work in the lifeless places of chaos and that the Spirit of God is hovering over and in those broken places. Samaria, where Jesus encountered a five-time-divorced Samaritan woman, who John tells us became the first evangelist, was a place you'd rather go around than through. Samaria was for "those" half-breed, "other-side-of-tracks" folks. The bigotry was both racial and religious in nature. Yet Jesus specifically includes Samaria in his list of places that Spirit-empowered, neighboring Christ-followers are to go. Before his ascension, Jesus commissioned his followers with this charge: "But you will receive power when the Holy Spirit comes upon you. And you will be my witnesses, telling people about me everywhere—in Jerusalem, throughout Judea, in Samaria, and to the ends of the earth" (Acts 1:8).

In our terms, Jerusalem would be our city or county, and Judea our state or country. The ends of the earth, of course, is everywhere else. Samaria, on the other hand, doesn't have a precise equivalent. It's the people in places we'd normally like to avoid, such as prisons, seedy bars, strip clubs, halfway houses, nursing homes, and blighted parts of our city. It's in these places, filled with pain and chaos, that God's Spirit is hovering.

In our book *A Grace Full Life,* [22] Wes Olds and I told a story about teaching at a Methodist seminary in Costa Rica. We were invited there to teach several dozen Costa Rican pastors. One morning we were teaching on the subject of God's prevenient grace. We told story after story of people at Grace Church whom Jesus had found in the wildest of places. From strip clubs to bars, we did our level best to convince them of God's activity "even there." In Spanish, the phrase for "even there" is *asta aye.* Over and over again, we would say, "El Senor esta asta aye," which means "The Lord is even there." Despite our insistence, the pastors were not convinced and kept saying back to us, "No. El Senor no esta asta aye," which translated, "No, the Lord is not even there." You see, their theology taught them that God could never be in hellish places like strip clubs and bars. God was too holy for that.

In the back of the room, there was one guy who didn't look like he belonged in the group. He wore a Harley-Davidson t-shirt, a leather jacket, and jeans. He was covered with tattoos and had a beard. After a while, he asked for permission to speak. He then told the class his story of walking out of a bar one night in Mexico and encountering a bunch of Christians who witnessed to him about God's love and gave him a tract, a little pamphlet that explained how to start a relationship with God. The man grabbed the tract, shoved it in his backpack, pushed the crowd aside, and jumped on his Harley and left.

Months later this same man was at the end of his rope. Filled with despair and darkness, he sat at a bar in Costa Rica to drink what he planned to be his last drink of rum. He walked upstairs to his room above the bar and sat on his bed. He reached in his backpack to grab his gun and kill himself, but instead pulled out the tract. He began to read in the little pamphlet about a God who loved him right where he was and who sent his Son to die on the cross so that his sins could be forgiven. Tears streamed down his face as that hardened biker became a follower of Jesus. Then he said to the pastors in training at the seminary, "El Senor esta asta aye." "The Lord is even there!" With that, the room erupted in praise and adoration of the God about whom Isaiah said, "Surely the arm of the Lord is not too short to save . . ." (Isaiah 59:1, NIV). Followers of Jesus who neighbor others know that God goes before us as we join God's mission.

MINISTRY IN THE MARKETPLACE

During his mission in Athens, Paul added "market-place" ministry to his strategic repertoire along with "synagogue" ministry. In the synagogue, Paul focused on all the things he had in common with Jewish people because of his heritage; but in the marketplace, Paul would have to lean into his Roman upbringing. Eventually, Paul finds himself speaking to the Aeropagus, a type of city council where city leaders gathered for debates. Here is how Luke records Paul's words:

*So Paul, standing before the council,
addressed them as follows: "Men of Athens, I
notice that you are very religious in every way,
for as I was walking along I saw your many
shrines. And one of your altars had this inscription on it: 'To an Unknown God.' This God,
whom you worship without knowing, is the one
I'm telling you about" (Acts 17:22-23).*

Paul begins engaging with these prominent Greek leaders by telling them about his experience while visiting Athens. His first move as a missionary who wanted to be a neighbor to the local people was to walk around the city. He became a student of their culture.

I suggest that we, as twenty-first-century followers of Jesus, should begin likewise. Instead of coming into our communities with both gospel barrels blazing, we should take a cue from the greatest missionary to ever live.

Paul looked,
Paul listened,
and Paul learned.

From this humble posture, he was able to engage in a spiritual conversation with the Greeks on their turf and in their language.

Instead of decrying their idolatry, he harnessed it as an opportunity for thoughtful conversation about God. In verses 24–31, it's interesting to note that Paul never actually mentions Jesus. He never quotes the Old Testament, because the Old Testament wasn't familiar to the Greeks. Even when he mentions God, it's in a generic way. Instead, he quotes one of their poets and allows that to become a common ground for the gospel. I believe as Paul walked around the city, as he looked, listened, and learned about the people and their culture, he was asking, "Where is the pain?"

In 1 Corinthians 9 Paul describes theologically what he illustrated practically in Acts 17. In a lengthy treatise, Paul defends himself and his team as those who have been given spiritual authority. Near the end of his argument, Paul describes what he has done to win them and others to Jesus. It's as part of this argument that he pens these famous words: "I have become all things to all people so that by all possible means I might save some" (1 Corinthians 9:22b).

When I was in seminary, my evangelism professor said, "When you go fishing for fish, you put on the hook what the fish like not what you like." Similarly, Craig Groeschel has echoed Paul when he says of his church, "We will do anything short of sin to reach people who don't know Christ."[23]

"Whatever it takes," you can hear Paul declare, "All things to all people so that by all means." Three times he uses a superlative. All means all. Years ago I was studying this text when one of my pastor colleagues at Grace Church, Kevin Griffin, came into my office. I told him I was studying this section of 1 Corinthians 9 and I'll never forget what Kevin said in response, while peering over my shoulder:

> *The Pharisee says, "You become like me to be saved," while the "incarnational" missional follower of Jesus says, "I'm going to become like you so that you might be saved."*

Eureka! Kevin nailed it! He was affirming what I call the elasticity of the gospel found in the power of the Holy Spirit. The good news of Jesus will shape itself to whatever context it finds itself.

THE IMPORTANCE OF CONTEXT

Let's think about how to put Paul's model of looking, listening, and learning into practice in the local twenty-first-century church. From personal experience, one of the principles we seek to live by at Grace Church is that vital congregations understand their context. Context for a local church can be defined as the clear picture of current reality, both internally and externally.

One of the things my team has learned in turning around existing churches and restarting closed congregations is that local churches are like addicts. They love denial! Comfortable with the status quo, the church can be lulled into believing "all is well," when the reality is far from it.

Here are a few examples. When I came to Grace Church in September of 1996, we had 1,000 members but less than 400 people attending worship, very few ministries for adults, students, and children, and no outreach ministries to the community or the world. Nevertheless, many leaders at the time believed all things were well.

In my first meeting with leadership during my first week as their pastor, I shared with the 38 men and women gathered in our fellowship hall that our average worship attendance had declined from 575 to less than 400 over the past five years. Many seemed shocked. A few shook their heads in disbelief, a handful nodded along in agreement and, sadly, some appeared not even to care. One leader spoke up and said, "We are declining because the District planted two new churches near us." Being 36 years old and not as seasoned as I am now, I quickly retorted, "You mean the one with 20 in attendance or the one with

200 eighty-year-olds!" The truth was that our congregation was filled with wonderful people who had
slowly drifted off mission with Jesus.

One more church denial story: My colleague Wes
Olds and I were invited to a wonderful midwestern city
to speak at a weekend leaders retreat. On Saturday
morning about twenty-five staff and leaders gathered in the conference room of a business owned by
one of their members. At some point, Wes and I were
describing our recovery ministries that reach hundreds
of people each week with hope and healing through
Jesus Christ. One of the leaders spoke up and said,
"Well that's fine and dandy for you in Florida, but we
don't have those kind of drug problems here in our
city." As fate had it, we had read in the local newspaper that morning a report about a handful of students
who had been arrested for using crystal meth in that
very city. Wes responded, "Did you read the paper this
morning?" Not much else needed to be said.

Church leaders need to be like the leaders
described in 1 Chronicles 12:32: "From the tribe of
Issachar, there were 200 leaders of the tribe with their
relatives. All these men understood the signs of the
times and knew the best course for Israel to take."

These men "understood the signs of the times and
knew the best course for Israel to take." Church leaders must be ruthlessly honest about both the internal
assets and liabilities of their church while simultane-
ously honing an acute sense of the real condition of
their community.

Think about the prophet Nehemiah. While in exile
in Persia, he received word that the walls around
Jerusalem had been torn down. He was heartsick at
this news so, after praying, he boldly approached the

king asking for permission and resources to rebuild the torn-down walls of the City of David. Surprisingly, Nehemiah received approval and the financial backing to fulfill his God-given assignment. I particularly love the next detail that the Bible gives in Nehemiah 2:11-15:

> So I arrived in Jerusalem. Three days later, I slipped out during the night, taking only a few others with me. I had not told anyone about the plans God had put in my heart for Jerusalem. We took no pack animals with us except the donkey I was riding. After dark I went out through the Valley Gate, past the Jackal's Well, and over to the Dung Gate to inspect the broken walls and burned gates. Then I went to the Fountain Gate and to the King's Pool, but my donkey couldn't get through the rubble. So, though it was still dark, I went up the Kidron Valley instead, inspecting the wall before I turned back and entered again at the Valley Gate.

Before building a team to fulfill God's mission and announcing the God-honoring project to them, Nehemiah does a walk around the city to assess the damage. Like Paul walking around Athens, Nehemiah walks around Jerusalem to get the lay of the land. He did an audit of the community.

Over the past twelve years at Grace Church, Spiritual Leadership, Inc. (SLI: www.spiritual-leadership.org), a walk-alongside coaching ministry, has given us tools to make an accurate internal and external assessment of our different campuses. This is especially important because the communities where our four campuses are located are vastly different and each has unique pains and possibilities. Over the years, SLI has helped us with both internal and external contextualizing for our multisite ministry.

The demographics of a community is the kind of information that savvy leaders use to shape their understanding of context. MissionInsite (*www.missioninsite.com*) is a remarkable online tool to gather reams of information on the communities surrounding a local church. From per family income to interest in spiritual matters, you can learn accurate and up-to-date information about your very real neighbors.

Simply walking and driving around the church's community with "new eyes" is another relatively easy discipline leaders can use to gain understanding of their context. Familiarity tends to breed contempt, and sometimes our proximity to a church and a community blinds us from the very communities we seek to reach for Christ.

SLI also taught us about the life cycle of a church. People, groups, businesses, and churches all have a life cycle. The stages they follow from birth to infancy to adolescence to adulthood to aging to death are almost unbreakable. A simple exercise to determine if a local church is aware and honest about where they are in a life cycle is to give everyone a simple life-cycle diagram (see diagram below) and ask them this question: Where is our church on our life cycle?

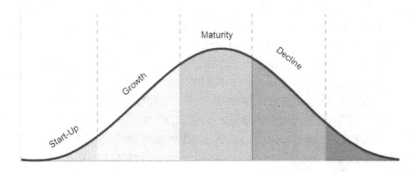

It's striking to see how many church leaders are living in denial in comparison with how many have an accurate, contextual understanding of where their congregation is in the cycle.

Sometimes when I am working with church leaders, I will use what I call "The church hell/church heaven" assessment tool (see diagram below). I'll say something like: "Think of the best church you can imagine as church heaven and the absolute worst church you can imagine as church hell. Where is your church on this continuum?"

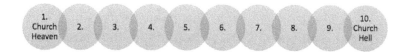

Again, the idea with all these tools is to get church leaders to assess accurately their congregation's relative vitality or lack of vitality, as well as revealing the rich possibilities for new ministry opportunities in the community. This is the process through which a local church can find and name the places of pain both within and outside of their congregation.

In this holy work of contextualizing and assessment, there are some driving principles to keep in mind. First, to capture current reality there must be a willingness to look as objectively as possible at the current situation. Denial, soft selling, and overstating do not help. As much objectivity as possible is essential.

Second, assigning blame will get you nowhere. The purpose of looking, listening, and learning is to find a new future not bemoan the failed past. Remember that assigning blame is reflective of our fallen nature as human beings and not of our redeemed nature as those who live in Christ. After the whole fruit-eating business, Adam and Eve began the blame game and it got them nowhere, the same place it gets us (Genesis 3:8-13).

Third, everyone has a stake in what is happening. From the charter member to the person in the community who does not yet know the love of Jesus and the gift of Christian community, everyone involved has skin in the game. In this work, all must be represented and all must have a voice.

Fourth, if there is a problem, everyone is affected by it. Again, from the saintliest to the most sinful, the problem is the problem and solving it affects everyone for the better.

Finally, all who have a stake in the future must participate. Several years ago, at the original campus of Grace Church, we observed that the congregation was aging with me. I had started with Grace at age 36 and twenty years later, when I was 56, the congregation looked more like me than my son and daughter-in-law. By most church standards in our denomination, we were still spring chickens, but we knew that to have a future filled with hope, we had to reach the next generations: the millennials and Gen Zers. A short-term team made up of mostly young adults was formed, and they were ruthless in their honesty. Frankly, we needed to hear it. Many of the recommendations we accepted. A few were not. Even though it hurt, these young adults had a stake in our future so they needed to fully participate in the assessment.

THE RESULTS IN ATHENS

As humans, we like results. So, it stands to reason that we want to know how it went for Paul after his no-Jesus-mentioning sermon to the city council. Here is Luke's report:

> When they heard Paul speak about the resurrection of the dead, some laughed in contempt, but others said, "We want to hear more about this later." That ended Paul's discussion with them, but some joined him and became believers. Among them were Dionysius, a member of the council, a woman named Damaris, and others with them (Acts 17:32-34).

Luke tells us about three responses from those who heard Paul's new strategy of spreading the good news in the marketplace:

- Some laughed.

- Some were interested and wanted to hear more.

- Some became followers of Jesus.

This sounds like every week at Grace Church and probably at just about any church. Some folks are just not buying what we are selling. Some have had their interest peaked, but they want to check it out more. And some, by the grace and mercy of God, step up to the line and surrender their lives to Jesus. Paul experienced what Jesus predicted would happen when gospel seed is slung (Matthew 13:1-23; Mark 4:1-20; and Luke 8:4-15). Some seed lands in good soil and other seed lands in soil not yet conducive to growth.

One of the innovations of the early Methodists was their discipling strategy. They created relational spaces with spiritual mentors that mirrored people's journey of grace. United Societies were gatherings of people who were experiencing God's prevenient or seeking grace. When a person indicated interest in further exploration of their faith, the early Methodist leaders created smaller Class Meetings of ten to twelve people with leaders who would help participants experience God's justifying grace. Once a person came to faith in Christ, they were put in a Band that was even smaller, around four to six people of the same gender, and focused on deeper community with the tasks of mutual accountability and watching over one another in love.

As I researched this further, I discovered that when a person who was not a Christian joined a Class Meeting, it took an average of three years for that person to come to faith in Christ. The early Methodists created a time, a space, and a community for those who did not yet believe in Jesus to come to faith. One question you might ask about your church is: Where is it safe to not be a Christian in our church?

IS IT NEWS TO ANYONE?

One of my dearest friends, Max Wilkins, is the president and CEO of a mission agency. He travels all over the world encouraging and training cross-cultural workers from North America as well as indigenous mission partners. Once, when Max was in India, he was invited to accompany Raj Kumar, an Indian evangelist, to a rural village that Kumar had been working with for several months. "Pastor Max," Raj said, "we have been going there for many months getting ready for this trip. We will be presenting the gospel, and I would very much like for you to be there with us." It was an offer too good to refuse so Max went along with Raj and the team.

As they were driving to the remote village, their Muslim driver said, "You know the villagers think your God is a powerful God." Raj responded, "Well, yes, my God is a powerful God, but why do the villagers think so?" To which the driver responded, "This is rainy season, and you've been speaking for eight weeks during monsoon season, but every time you show up, it does not rain." Raj replied, "This might not be good."

When the group arrived at the village, they quickly got to work setting up a sound system when Max noticed, far on the horizon, a small dark cloud racing across the sky. Within minutes that small cloud had grown and covered the skies from horizon to horizon and a downpour began to flood the village. The cloud cover had detonated like a bomb in the middle of the village, and all the villagers ran to find cover in their homes.

Everyone except Raj Kumar. He threw his arms wide and began to pray loudly: "This is Satan. Jesus, this is not your will. Jesus, in your name, stop this rain." And with that the rain settled down to a drizzle. Max humorously thought to himself, *Now would be a good time to take an offering.* Instead Raj Kumar looked up at the drizzling sky, dropped on his knees in the center of the village and, with his face inches from the rain-soaked ground, he raised his hands towards the heavens and shouted: "No, God! You are not a God who does things halfway. In the name of Jesus Christ, stop this rain!" The rain stopped completely. The sun began to shine on that little village, the villagers came out of their huts, and that day people gave their lives to Jesus by the droves.

On the way home, Max turned to Raj and said: "Raj, you are a powerful man of God. I don't see these kinds of things in America."

Without hesitation, Raj responded: "Pastor Max, I am not a powerful man. I am poor and uneducated. I don't even have the respect of my own people. I have no power. Now my God is a powerful God. You know why you don't see things like that?"

Max answered, "No, why?"

"You don't see things like that because you don't preach the gospel!"

Taken back by his assessment, Max said, "Well, Raj. I've been a preacher for a while, and I do think I preach the gospel."

"I know you do, Max, but that's the problem," replied Raj. "What is the gospel, Pastor Max?" continued Raj.

"Well, it's the good news of Jesus Christ," Max replied.

"Would you say it's always good?"

Max thought about it for a moment and said, "Yes, it's always good."

"I would too. We are on the same page," Raj Kumar continued. "Now, here's the question. Is it always news?"

Raj continued: "Max, here's what you do in the United States. You gather the already convinced and make the pastor go over the story every week to make sure it hasn't changed. And then you come back next week and do the same thing all over again." Then Raj peered at Max and asked, "Do you know what Romans 1:16 says?"

Max replied, "For I am not ashamed of the gospel, because it is the power of God . . . ."

Raj interrupted Max: "Stop. Did you hear what you just said? The gospel of Jesus Christ is the power of God. Listen to me because this is the point. If you'll get busy taking the good news not to just where it is good but to where it is also news, you will unleash the power of God."

Friends, we must ask ourselves this question every day: Are we taking the gospel of Jesus Christ to the people in our community for whom the gospel is both good and news? It was both good and news for those people with whom Paul shared in Athens. It was both good and news for that small rural village in India visited by Raj Kumar and Max. And it was both good and news to the poor of England in the 1700s. Neighboring followers of Jesus must find places of pain in their community where the gospel is both "good" and "news" and watch God unleash God's healing power.

Questions for Personal Reflection and Group Discussion

1. What does the story of John Wesley and George Whitefield preaching in the fields teach us about reaching our neighbors? How can your church get out in the community to reach people who won't hear the good news in traditional settings?

2. Where is there pain in your community? How can you and your fellow followers of Jesus be on the lookout for places of pain where you can help out?

3. In what ways do we shape the gospel message for our modern context? How can we change our methods to share the good news with people in contexts that are unfamiliar?

4. What does it mean for the good news of Jesus to be both "good" and "news"? How can we make sure the gospel is both when we are sharing it with others?

CHAPTER THREE
A Neighbored Christian

You cannot give what you do not have. —Unknown

When I was growing up as a teenager in Orlando, Florida, my parents had strict expectations. You could say they ran a tight ship. I knew better than to come to breakfast unless my bed was made, my towel was hung up in the bathroom, and my clean clothes were put away. I also knew that, before I ran around our neighborhood wreaking havoc on Saturday with my best friends Alex and David, I had to finish my morning chores. These chores included mowing and edging the yard in the era before weed whackers were invented! It also meant washing the cars and any other duties assigned by my Mom and Dad.

Saturday afternoons included another family ritual. After finishing chores and having some fun with my buddies, most late Saturday afternoons were spent in our den with my dad watching one of our favorite shows, ABC's *Wide World of Sports*. I remember that each episode always began with the same familiar phrase spoken over orchestral music, "The thrill of victory and the agony of defeat!"

That phrase isn't just applicable to sports; it's true of everything. Years ago one of my mentors taught me that life is "iffy." Life has a big I-F in the middle of it.

Jesus himself acknowledges it in the Gospel of John: "I have told you all this so that you may have peace in me. Here on earth you will have many trials and sorrows. But take heart, because I have overcome the world" (John 16:33).

Jesus did not say, "We *might* experience trials and sorrows." He didn't say, "We *could* experience trials and sorrows." Jesus didn't even say, "We *should* experience trials and sorrows." Jesus said, "You *will* have trials and sorrows." Not just that, but "*many* trials and sorrows." It's safe to say that not every day walking with Jesus will be filled with the thrill of victory. We all will have our share of days marked by the agony of defeat.

For me and my family, Monday, October 16, 2016, was one of those "agony of defeat" days. I was at Camp Sumatonga, the camp facility for the North Alabama Annual Conference of The United Methodist Church, along with two of my Grace Church pastoral colleagues, Shari and Wes. The previous evening I had given the opening message to the "Gathering of the Orders," a group of several hundred pastors in the North Alabama Conference. In that message I was able to share the amazing story of what God had done at our local church back in Southwest Florida. The following morning our team was excited to get busy and lead five more sessions with the pastors over the next day and a half.

As we sat drinking coffee, Shari was checking her e-mail using the camp Wi-Fi. With a very serious tone, Shari looked up at me and said: "Jorge, you need to call the office. There's been an accident with Zoe." Zoe was my eighteenth-month-old granddaughter and the fourth child of my son Daniel and his wife Courtney.

There were no additional details in the e-mail from our office, and the camp was so far out in the "sticks" that there was no cell phone reception. My heart was beating out of my chest. Thankfully, I remembered that I could video chat with my wife using the Wi-Fi. When her face appeared, she was sobbing.

"What happened?" I asked.

"Courtney ran over Zoe with the car."

"Is she alive?" I responded, shocked.

"I don't know. I'm on my way to the hospital now. I'll call you," Cheryl sobbed.

And with that the screen went blank. I fell to my knees and began to cry from the depths of my soul. I felt like I was either going to pass out or vomit.

The next few hours were a blur. Shari drove me from the camp to the Atlanta airport, a two-hour trip. Zoe and Courtney were airlifted by a helicopter from Fort Myers to Tampa General Hospital, where a pediatric neurological team would tend to our precious Zoe. I only vaguely remember the plane flight from Atlanta to Tampa. The following days were filled with tense moments and agonized anticipation as we waited to receive the test results on our beautiful granddaughter.

Today, I am glad to report that Zoe is alive and doing remarkably well. Miraculously, she left the hospital only seven days later. Serendipitously, doctors discovered from one of Zoe's MRI's that she had a chiari malformation, completely unrelated to the accident, that was causing our little girl extreme pain, especially as she slept. A simple surgery has repaired this as well.

We've all had days like this, days filled with crisis and fear and anxiety. What happens when these days come into your life? What do you do when things go sideways and your life gets iffy? How do you prepare for the days when the bad diagnosis is delivered? How do you respond when your child becomes lost in the devilish world of addictions, or when your employer sits you down to tell you that you no longer have a place in the company? How do you handle these "agony of defeat" days?

We face these questions in ministry too. How do we support our neighbors, our community, and our world during these tough days? When the wheels come off, how can we, as faithful followers of Jesus, stay on mission? There have been many days over my thirty years in ministry when the sorrows of life simply overwhelmed and overshadowed the demands of my work. How does one move forward in faithful and fruitful ministry in the face of these defeats?

LIVE DIFFERENTLY

There are many possible answers to the question, but the one that tops my list is that we must live differently. We catch a glimpse of this call to live differently in Paul's letter to the followers of Jesus who were living under the powerful empire of Rome.

Let me remind you that Paul and the first followers of Jesus were living in an empire that was ruled by Nero, a homicidal, genocidal, ruthlessly violent maniac. If you take a quick look at Nero's biography, you'll discover he murdered his own mother, set Rome on fire and blamed followers of Jesus for it, then executed the Christians by throwing them to the beasts, crucifying them, and burning them. Paul and his companions understood a thing or two about dealing with people who committed atrocious acts and the agony they inflict. To these beaten down, worn-out Christ-followers, Paul gives the following encouragement to live differently in Romans 12:1-2:

"And so, dear brothers and sisters, I plead with you to give your bodies to God because of all he has done for you. Let them be a living and holy sacrifice—the kind he will find acceptable. This is truly the way to worship him. Don't copy the behavior and customs of this world, but let God transform you into a new person by changing the way you think. Then you will learn to know God's will for you, which is good and pleasing and perfect."

Paul invites those who might be tempted to jettison the faith because of hardship to live differently by resisting the tug of culture. He tells them not to "copy the behaviors and customs of this world." This is a call to live differently.

In THE MESSAGE translation of the Bible by the much loved and now departed Eugene Peterson, verse 2a, "Don't copy the behavior and customs of this world, but let God transform you into a new person by changing the way you think" is translated this way: "Unlike the culture around you, always dragging you down to its level of immaturity, God brings the best out of you, develops well-formed maturity in you."

We live in a culture, particularly in North America, that glamorizes rugged individualism. Our society is highly independent. We like to tell ourselves that we are a "pull yourselves up by your own bootstraps" kind of people.

A year ago, my wife Cheryl and I were in Chicago, and we decided to see Lin Manuel-Miranda's award-winning musical *Hamilton*. If you aren't familiar, the musical tells the story of one of America's founding fathers, Alexander Hamilton. As we watched, we realized all the ways that our American conception of rugged individualism was woven into the fabric of our national identity even at its birth.

Now that's not all bad. I get it. It helped free us from the tyranny of Great Britain, but it also has enslaved us to an unhealthy sense of self-reliance. I believe the enemy of our soul, the devil, knows this and capitalizes on it to our spiritual demise. You see, as long as the devil keeps us isolated from others and reliant upon ourselves, we do not live into our Creator's intent for us and Satan wins. But, in rich, genuine Christian community, we can do what the early Methodists did and "watch over one another in love." [24]

In a sense, Christian community is kind of like the Promised Land for followers of Jesus. In community, we embrace our God-given need for others. It is the land flowing with milk and honey, because in Christian community we create space for other followers of Jesus to help us grow in our relationship with God. In community, neighbors are neighbored themselves. It's in community that we are free to ask one another, "How is it with your soul?" It's in community that we invite a trusted few to help us stay faithful in our most important relationships. Do a self-inventory. Ask yourself these questions:

- Who are my spiritual partners that help me with my relationship with God?

- Who are my spiritual partners that help me with my relationship with myself?

- Who are my spiritual partners that help me with my relationship with others?

If the answers to these questions don't come to mind quickly, maybe it's time to reevaluate your relational life and make some changes. Here's the deal, the journey to the Promised Land of Christian community begins just like it did for the enslaved Hebrews more than three thousand years ago in the land of slavery, a deep and dark place of isolation. It may take some time to move through the land in between, and it can be difficult to traverse the desert wilderness to arrive in the promised land of rich, deep, and genuine community—but there is joy to be found in the journey.

This is what it means and what it takes to live differently. Culture wins when we try live a heroic solo life, and we find ourselves "dragged down to its level of immaturity."

MATH AND COMMUNITY

From elementary school all the way through seminary, I excelled in English, literature, history, and the arts, but I struggled in math and science. It was always hard work for me to memorize all those laws and formulas. I even remember coming to tears when trying to learn my multiplication tables in the third grade. Even as a grandfather, I still struggle with it. Thank goodness my cell phone has a calculator!

But one thing I do remember about math came from my geometry classes. So, let's do some geometry. First, let me put you at ease: there won't be a pop quiz at the end of this exercise. It will be simple because I'm not interested in teaching about the laws of math but instead the laws of the Spirit.

In geometry I learned about lines. Now, lines can divide us, but this isn't always bad. Regularly, my wife and I take our grandkids to Disney World, the happiest and most expensive place on earth! As we stand in those hellishly long queues at Disney, they have stanchions that keep us orderly. Lines work to keep order. This is a good thing.

But I think you'd agree with me that lines also can separate us in negative ways. Sometimes our lines are not like the orderly ones at Disney and meant to enhance our experience; instead there are dividing lines we draw in our hearts and minds. Sometimes in life, we draw lines to keep "us" separated from "them." Sometimes these lines are relatively insignificant, like whether your favorite football team is Alabama or Georgia. Other times we draw lines based on more important things, like which political party someone votes for or a person's nation of origin. We also draw lines based on skin color, marital status, social issues, and even which church you attend, or if you attend church at all. These lines tend to divide us sharply.

But in geometry, I also learned about circles. Now, circles can be used to keep people in or out, but for our purposes, let me suggest that circles can be radically inclusive because circles can be expanded to include more and more people. Circles are significantly more inclusive than lines.

What I'm about to say can be misunderstood easily, so please hear me carefully. I love what we do when we gather for worship in our local churches. I love the feeling of God's people worshiping and learning together. But there is a downside to it. Sadly, many of us believe that all our spiritual needs will be met by sitting in neat rows watching and listening to the choir, the worship band, and the pastor. While I believe that weekly worship is essential for spiritual growth, it's just not all there is to worship. Far too many followers of Jesus put all their spiritual-growth eggs in the Sunday morning worship basket.

In the last few years, a new mantra has emerged within the church I lead: *Miracles most often happen in circles not rows.* Rows of chairs and pews are lines. God has done and will continue to do miraculous work in our churches as we sit in rows week after week; but as wonderful and important as weekly worship is to us, God seems to do God's best work in and through us when we circle up. In circles we don't see the back of a person's head. Instead we are knee-to-knee and can see the glimmer in one another's eyes. Miracles most often happen in circles not rows. In circles I can know and be known. I can love and be loved. I can correct and be corrected. The list goes on and on.

One of the principles of the spiritual life that I teach at Grace Church has to do with living preventatively rather than prescriptively. Prescriptive living means that when I get sick I go to the doctor, but it also means I do very little to avoid getting sick. The doctor will give me medicine and help me get better, but if I do things like eating well, exercising, and getting adequate sleep before I get sick, I may never need the doctor. Here's what this means for the spiritual life:

> *What I do during days of peace and serenity will determine how I manage days of conflict and chaos.*

This is what it means to live a preventative spiritual life. "Agony of defeat" days are coming. There always will be some "iffy" days in a calendar year for us. Jesus said so. One of the best ways to live preventatively is not only to be a neighbor but also to be neighbored by others.

There is yet another aspect of this call to live differently in rich and deep communities and it's this:

*The degree to which we live faithfully
inwardly will determine the degree to which we
will reach fruitfully outwardly.*

Followers of Jesus must embody neighborly living. This becomes one of our witnesses to a broken world.

When I arrived at Grace Church in 1996, one of the first things I did was start a men's small group. At the outset, I invited about ten men to join me. We would meet from 6 to 7:15 a.m. to study the Bible and pray for one another. Twenty-plus years later, we still meet at my home on Tuesday mornings at 6:00 a.m. We have laughed and cried together. Members of our group have died, and we eulogized them together. We end each morning by gathering in a circle as each man prays.

I've often wondered through the years, *What do my neighbors think?* Recently one of them, a salty, retired parole officer, made a comment about our group. He was preparing to move out of the neighborhood and he told me in his gruff voice, "I'm coming over for your men's group before I leave." The winsome witness of ten men driving their cars to our home every Tuesday morning at 5:50 a.m. had stirred something in my neighbor. Living differently in community is a witness too.

FAITHFULNESS BEFORE FRUITFULNESS

When I was young, our living room at home was an off-limits room. Kids were only "invited" into this room. The room was pristine with beautiful furniture, exotic wall-hangings, and souvenirs my father had collected from his travels around the world. On one table sat a beautiful bowl of fruit that I had long admired from afar. One day I could no longer resist the temptation. When my mom wasn't looking, I stealthily made my way into the forbidden zone of the living room.

I gingerly stepped on the carpet as if I were walking through a field of land mines. Quietly, I approached the bowl of fruit and gently lifted a beautiful apple from the bowl and held it up in front of my face. It looked so delicious that I did the unthinkable. I took a bite. Sure enough, it was a waxy, artificial apple! Embarrassed, I carefully placed the apple back in the bowl, teeth marks down. Only decades later did I, like Adam and Eve before their Creator, admit my apple-biting ways to my mom.

I wonder how many of us are living a life for Christ that's like my mom's bowl: full of artificial fruit. We look like the real deal. We go to church, attend Sunday school, serve on committees and boards, and engage in religious conversations—but truth be told, we're kind of faking it. For example, in one of the more disappointing commentaries on the American church, most Christians see faith-sharing as the responsibility of the local church and not as their individual responsibility. This is bad theology (we are all the church), as well as bad Christian practice (faith-sharing is the work of all God's people).

The Barna Group reports that in 1993 only 10 percent of Christians who had shared about their faith agreed with the statement "converting people to Christianity is the job of the local church" and not the job of an individual. In 2018, 29 percent of Christians agreed with the same statement.

The report goes on to comment: "This jump could be the result of many factors, including poor ecclesiology (believing 'the local church' is somehow separate from the people who are a part of it) or personal and cultural barriers to sharing faith. Yet the most dramatic divergence over time is on the statement, 'Every Christian has a responsibility to share their faith.' In 1993, nine out of 10 Christians who had shared their faith agreed (89%). Today, just two-thirds say so (64%)—a 25-point drop."[25]

Sharing the good news is not optional according to Jesus. Joining Jesus in his work of fishing for men and women is not recreational. Jesus' last recorded words in all four Gospel narratives, as well as the Book of Acts, charge ordinary followers of Jesus with joining Jesus in his mission to the world (Matthew 28:18-20; Mark 16:15; Luke 24:44-49; John 20:19-23; Acts 1:8). Somehow many American followers of Jesus see this as somebody else's assignment.

I love the metaphor that Jesus used in John 15 when he described the organic relationship that followers of Jesus have with our triune God. God the Father is described by Jesus as the gardener (John 15:1) who tends to the vineyard, and Jesus is the vine who transports the unnamed Holy Spirit "sap" to the branches (John 15:5). Our connection to God creates the possibility of Kingdom fruit. Jesus uses the phrase "much fruit" to describe the yield from followers of Jesus who are connected to him. In John 15, Jesus teaches us the following Kingdom principle: *Faithfulness to God precedes fruitfulness for God.*

Could it be that our lack of fruitfulness in the American church is directly connected to a lack of faithfulness? I first learned in the rooms of recovery that you cannot give what you do not have. That may be why so many followers of Jesus see evangelism as somebody else's job. Faith only flows from a follower of Jesus who is vitally connected to Jesus.

Faithfulness to God requires community. Let this sink in. The "you" that Jesus speaks of in John 15 is not in the second person singular in Greek, but rather the second person plural. So when Jesus says, "You are the branches" in John 15:5, he's literally saying, "You all are the branches" or, as my friends in the deep South say, "Y'all." Jesus' invitation to vital faithfulness in God and fruitfulness through God is an invitation to live in Christian community.

There's an oft-repeated line from John Wesley that goes, "There is no holiness but social holiness." That quote is usually used to argue that social action is squarely in the center of what it means to be holy and therefore social action is necessary and proper for followers of Jesus. While the conclusion may be true, the quote is often taken out of context. Here's the exact quote from Wesley:

> Directly opposite to this [the approach of the desert mystics] is the gospel of Christ. Solitary religion is not to be found there. "Holy solitaries" is a phrase no more consistent with the gospel than holy adulterers. The gospel of Christ knows no religion, but social; no holiness but social holiness. [26]

According to John Wesley, social holiness is not about drilling wells in Africa or opening a food pantry for the poor. Those are all good things that followers of Jesus should do, but that's not the point Wesley was making. Instead, Wesley was advocating for Christians to live in community with one another.

Wesley's oft misused quote is a condemnation of private, individualized, personalized, separated-from-the-body, solitary religion. The early Methodist system of United Societies, Classes, and Bands was developed for people all along the spiritual journey to find a place, a people, and a process to help them experience God's grace. From seekers to new believers to growing saints, these early Methodists found and walked in grace while living in community. I've gone as far as telling my tribe, "Don't call yourself a Methodist if you are not in a small group!"

THE PROTOTYPE CHURCH

The word *prototype* describes a first attempt or preliminary model of something like a car or a cell phone. Prototypes set the standard for all the revisions and updated versions that go into creating the next generation of a product. The movement of Jesus had its own prototype church, which has been described to us by Luke in the Book of Acts. I like to teach our people that if Matthew, Mark, Luke, and John, the four Gospels, are the four biographies of the life of Jesus, then Acts is the biography of the Holy Spirit, highlighting the power and presence at work in and through Jesus' first apprentices.

Luke records that 120 followers of Jesus experienced the Holy Spirit in a fresh and new way. The Spirit of God that previously was given to select individuals was now given to all of Christ's followers. Quoting the Old Testament prophet Joel in Acts 2:17-18, Peter declares the scope of the Holy Spirit's invasion:

> *"In the last days," God says,*
> *"I will pour out my Spirit upon all people.*
> *Your sons and daughters will prophesy.*
> *Your young men will see visions.*
> *and your old men will dream dreams.*
> *In those days I will pour out my Spirit*
> *even on my servants—men and women alike—*
> *and they will prophesy."*

Women and men, young and old, will be empowered and equipped by the Holy Spirit to do Kingdom work, making the realities of heaven into the realities of earth. On that day, which we now call Pentecost, three thousand people chose to follow Jesus. That's some new member class! Luke goes on to describe the character of this fledgling missionary group. This is how they set the bar, the standard for all followers of Jesus: "All the believers devoted themselves to the apostles' teaching, and to fellowship, and to sharing in meals (including the Lord's Supper), and to prayer" (Acts 2:42).

These activities describe what it meant for the prototype gathering of neighbored Christ-followers to live differently. In the midst of huge challenges from both the overzealous Jewish leaders and the oppressive Roman Empire, Luke provides four spiritual practices that highlight ways this early missionary band lived life differently for others to see.

Luke tells us they were "devoted" to these four practices. To be devoted means to show steadfast strength and to continue working toward something with intense effort despite any difficulty. It takes commitment. It takes effort. This first community serves as the model for a whole new way of living. Instead of seeking to copy the dominant culture or fall in line with the latest fad, these first Christ-followers lived an entirely different life from the world around them. Together, more than three thousand people "devoted themselves" to imitating Jesus' life in this way.

These devoted followers of Jesus not only clung to the cross but also to one another. They knew that to live each day as a believer meant also becoming a belong-er. The grace of Jesus that cleanses us from sin also calls us into a new family, the body of Christ. To turn away from the culture also meant turning toward a new community. They realized they were better together.

WHY ARE WE BETTER TOGETHER?

Luke not only tells us how the prototype church practiced their faith but also what they did. Following are the four principles to which this community devoted itself.

1. The apostles' teaching
2. Fellowship
3. The breaking of bread
4. Prayer

But what is the "why" behind these four principles? Why did these first followers of Jesus focus on these four standards, and why are they still so important for us two thousand years later?

I believe that each of these four principles are important because they run counter to the prevailing culture of both the first and twenty-first centuries. When I use the word *culture* here, I mean the prevailing spirit or philosophy of the day. In John's five New Testament books (the Gospel of John, the Letters of 1, 2 and 3 John, and the Book of Revelation), he often uses the phrase "the world" to describe this culture that is contrary to the values of the Kingdom. For example, John writes:

> *Do not love this world nor the things it offers you, for when you love the world, you do not have the love of the Father in you. For the world offers only a craving for physical pleasure, a craving for everything we see, and pride in our achievements and possessions. These are not from the Father, but are from this world. And this world is fading away, along with everything that people crave. But anyone who does what pleases God will live forever (1 John 2:15-17).*

John is clearly not talking about trees, puppies, and cupcakes. These things are good, especially cupcakes, and are meant to be enjoyed. Rather, John uses the phrase "the world" to describe those things that are in stark contrast to the kingdom of God.

Sometimes when I visit the preschool at our church, I laugh to myself as I watch the three- and four-year-olds tussle over who gets to be the line leader to the restroom or the playground: "I want to be first!" "No, I want to be first!" Of course, adults have their versions of this fight too.

In Mark's Gospel, he tells a story in which Jesus has this "line leader" conversation with his disciples (Mark 10:35-45). James and John approach Jesus with a request. "When you establish your kingdom here" (code for "When you overthrow the Romans and establish yourself as the rightful ruler over Israel"), "can we sit in the places of honor on your right and left?" In essence, James and John are asking, "Can we be big shots once you've become the king? We want to be first in line!" Dr. Martin Luther King, Jr., called this line-leader impulse in all of us "the drum major instinct."[27] In my imagination, I can see Jesus hitting his head with the palm of his hand and saying "Oy-vey!" Mark gives us an amazing detail about what happened next:

When the ten other disciples heard what James and John had asked, they were indignant. So, Jesus called them together and said:

> *"You know that the rulers in this world lord it over their people, and officials flaunt their authority over those under them. But among you it will be different. Whoever wants to be a leader among you must be your servant, and whoever wants to be first among you must be*

*the slave of everyone else. For even the Son of
Man came not to be served but to serve oth-
ers and to give his life as a ransom for many"
(Mark 10:41-45).*

The other ten quickly became "indignant." Why?
Was it because they were aghast at this request for
power? I think not. I'm convinced it was because
James and John beat them to the punch. They wanted
to be the line leaders too. Far too often, so do I.
Jesus corrected the line-leader impulse found in his
first-century and twenty-first-century followers. He
tells us, "but among you it will be different" (verse
43a).

Jesus' people are a countercultural people. With
the help of the Holy Spirit and one another they seek
to love their enemies, do good to those who perse-
cute them, care for the forgotten, and stand up against
bullies. In a world obsessed with "worldly desires,"
followers of Jesus are called to be what Peter calls
"temporary residents and foreigners" (1 Peter 2:11).

Indeed, there is much in our world that is good, but
there is also a lot that is sick and broken. How else
do you explain genocides in Serbia, Syria, and South
Sudan? How else can we justify that God has given
our world enough food to feed the planet, but according to UNICEF approximately 3.1 million children still
die from undernutrition each year? (*www.worldhun-
ger.org/world-child-hunger-facts/*). Our beautiful, yet
broken world needs the redemption of Jesus. We are
called to be part of that redemption as the body and
bride of Christ.

As I mentioned before, the four spiritual practices
of community living described in Acts 2:42 worked

together to reject the prevailing culture of the day. Let's look at these practices one at a time.

1. They devoted themselves to the apostles' teaching.

First, together Christ's followers rejected a culture of lies. I've often heard the phrase "the apostles' teaching" defined as the Bible, but that would be functionally impossible. Remember, these are the first followers of Jesus. They aren't reading and studying the Bible as we know it. Instead, they are living the story the Bible will eventually tell us. The apostles' teaching that Luke describes were the stories of Jesus' remarkable birth, glorious life, controversial teaching, grisly death, and magnificent resurrection. The oral stories of Jesus told by his first followers were their guide.

Several years ago I was privileged to sit at a table for a day and a half with one of the premier New Testament scholars of our day, N.T. Wright. I took the cotton out of my ears and put it in my mouth for those two days and took lots of notes. At one point, I asked Dr. Wright this question: "What was the distinction of the first church?" His response was frankly predictable and confirming.

He said, "What distinguished the first followers of Jesus was their passionate love for one another and their reckless love for the poor and the diseased of the first century."

In a Roman culture that devalued human life, the dedication of Jesus' followers to the teachings of the apostles that emphasized the value and importance of loving and sharing with one another distinguished them. In Acts 4:32-35, Luke describes the passionate love for one another of the prototype church in this way:

All the believers were united in heart and mind. And they felt that what they owned was not their own, so they shared everything they had. The apostles testified powerfully to the resurrection of the Lord Jesus, and God's great blessing was upon them all. There were no needy people among them, because those who owned land or houses would sell them and bring the money to the apostles to give to those in need.

These followers of Jesus were living out the words of their Rabbi who challenges our inclinations to greed and consumerism. That challenge doesn't come only through his teaching but also through the way Jesus lived his life. The followers of Jesus lived an economically different life, rejecting the first-century culture of opulence and self-indulgence.

In Acts 6, Luke tells us that the movement of Jesus cared for so many of the poor in their community that the fledgling church had to establish a group of seven men to focus on the task of caring for the daily food service of the gathered. They had to appoint a team and create a system to manage the growth of the Jesus movement. Luke writes of these seven men and the expanding witness of the church in this way:

These seven were presented to the apostles, who prayed for them as they laid their hands on them. So God's message continued to spread. The number of believers greatly increased in Jerusalem, and many of the Jewish priests were converted, too (6:6-7).

The reckless love of Jesus' followers spilled out and embraced the poor of Jerusalem. Instead of being cast aside or thrown away, the poor and diseased were invited into the community, and through all of this, the church grew.

Our twenty-first-century American culture devalues life in much the same way as the first-century Roman culture did. The echoes of the apostles' teaching still beckon us to have, in the words of N.T. Wright, "passionate love for one another" and "reckless love for the poor and the diseased" of our day. This tension between "loving in" and "loving out" has been a kingdom dynamic of God's people for two thousand years.

Many years ago our high school students at Grace Church went on a mission trip to serve in Appalachia. While there, they served alongside a United Methodist Church that had begun a ministry for the poor and marginalized in their community. Each year, before school started in the fall, they gave away new shoes and backpacks to children and youth in their community. Our students were asked to join them and, when they came home, they had a vision for "Shoes of Hope" (*www.egracechurch.com/shoes/*; also see video at *www.youtube.com/watch?v=-pTZEU5iTeA*).

In the summer of 2011, this ministry was launched. Today, this ministry helps nearly nine hundred children at six sites, including a public elementary school. The most remarkable thing is that the children and families we help are not just from our community but also from our church. Often, we'll witness a mother and her children serve all day then, at the end of the day, get in line to be served themselves. We also are involved in ministry with two local elementary schools through mentoring and other opportunities, allowing us to have an ongoing relationship with these same families throughout the year. We believe that, when an ongoing relationship is added to the act of caring for others, it fulfills the model set by the prototype church who offered God's "reckless love" to the poor.

2. They devoted themselves to fellowship.

This second principle from Acts 2 tells us that together the first followers of Christ rejected a culture of isolation. The word *fellowship* comes from the Greek word *koinonia* which can also mean "joint participation" or "sharing something in common" (*www. bibletools.org/index.cfm/fuseaction/Lexicon.show/ID/ G2842/koinonia.htm*). It is a kind of sacred partnership that was expressed in their dedication to care for one another's needs.

How did our triune God reach this planet with God's love? Followers of Jesus wrestle with this central question. The easy answer is "through Jesus," but let's push a little deeper. What did Jesus do when he arrived on this planet? After three decades of quietly living as the son of Joseph and Mary in Nazareth, Jesus gathered a small group of followers (Luke 8:1-3). Jesus invested three years of his life in this ragtag group. He taught them how to live differently and modeled this Kingdom life for them with his own. Jesus didn't need a big tent or an expensive sound system to take his show on the road. He didn't need to start a new hip worship service to entertain his followers. He formed a small group, and he invested himself in this band of men and women, the same men and women who later would be filled with the Spirit and inspired to lead his movement forward. *Koinonia* was Jesus' vehicle for mission fulfillment.

Think theologically with me for a moment. What was the first crisis in the Bible? Many of us would say that the first crisis was when Adam and Eve ate the fruit from the forbidden tree. A moral crisis is most familiar to us.

But a more thorough look at the Creation story found in Genesis 2 reminds us that there was a crisis prior to this one. After Adam was shaped by God's hands and quickened by God's breath, God said to Adam, "It is not good for the man to be alone" (Genesis 2:18).

The first crisis in the Bible was not a moral crisis but a relational one. When God says that something is not good, it's not good. It's still not good for people to be alone. We were made by God, in the image of our triune God. It's part of God's nature to be in community, and we share that attribute. I am convinced that part of what it means to be an image-bearer is to live in community.

Early in 2018, several news agencies reported on the United Kingdom appointing a "minister for loneliness" to address the troubling trend towards isolation in Britain (*www.cnn.com/2018/01/17/health/uk-minister-loneliness-intl/index.html*). Our friends across the pond have discovered that loneliness not only affects the quality of life of British citizens but also shortens life expectancy, reduces the likelihood of regular exercise, encourages poor dietary habits, causes people to visit doctors less often, and leads to increases in stress, inflammation, blood pressure, and heart disease. *Koinonia* is God's remedy to many of these ailments.

Mother Teresa famously wrote these prophetic words:

> *The greatest disease in the West today is not TB or leprosy; it is being unwanted, unloved, and uncared for. We can cure physical diseases with medicine, but the only cure for loneliness, despair, and hopelessness is love. There are many in the world who are dying for a piece of bread but there are many more dying for a little*

love. The poverty in the West is a different kind of poverty—it is not only a poverty of loneliness but also of spirituality. There's a hunger for love, as there is a hunger for God. [28]

Fellow Roman Catholic writer and speaker Father Henri Nouwen wrote:

Loneliness is without a doubt one of the most widespread diseases of our time. It affects not only retired life but also family life, neighborhood life, school life, and business life. It causes suffering not only in elderly people but also in children, teenagers, and adults. It enters not only prisons but also private homes, office buildings, and hospitals. It is even visible in the diminishing interaction between people on the streets of our cities. Out of all this pervading loneliness many cry, "Is there anyone who really cares? Is there anyone who can take away my inner sense of isolation? Is there anyone with whom I can feel at home?" [29]

The answer to these questions is, "Yes." There are people who truly care; there are people who help us feel at home and embrace us. The first followers of Jesus showed us how to live differently with their rich expressions of communal love.

Recently, health insurer Cigna published a nationwide survey of 20,000 adults on the impact of loneliness in the United States and discovered some mind-bending findings about the toll of isolation in our country (*www.cigna.com/newsroom/news-releases/2018/new-cigna-study-reveals-loneliness-at-epidemic-levels-in-america*).

- Nearly half of Americans report sometimes or always feeling alone (46 percent) or left out (47 percent).

- One in four Americans (27 percent) rarely or never feel as though there are people who truly understand them.

- Two in five Americans sometimes or always feel that their relationships are not meaningful (43 percent) and that they are isolated from others (43 percent).

- One in five people report they rarely or never feel close to people (20 percent) or feel like there are people they can talk to (18 percent).

- Only around half of Americans (53 percent) have meaningful in-person social interactions, such as having an extended conversation with a friend or spending quality time with family on a daily basis.

- Generation Z (adults ages 18-22) is the loneliest generation and claims to be in worse mental health than older generations.

These are staggering findings, yet they are also useful insights for followers of Jesus who want to seriously impact our culture with the gospel of Jesus. People have a desperate longing to belong, and the people of God can tap into this longing for the glory of God and the good of others.

My daughter-in-law Courtney and son Daniel have both told me that their young couples' small group at Grace Church was their lifeline in the days following Zoe's accident. They provided care for Zoe and a hotel room for Courtney so she could get a good night's rest after several days sleeping in the hospital. They provided a car for Courtney to drive because of the trauma she associated with her car after Zoe's accident. They provided food and care for their other three children and, when the thousands of dollars of hospital bills came in, they even helped with money. Like the four friends who lowered their sick friend through a ceiling in front of Jesus, Courtney and Daniel's small group covered them in prayer before the God who heals. I love the line in Mark's telling of the story of the paralyzed man and his four friends: "Seeing their faith, Jesus said to the paralyzed man, 'My child, your sins are forgiven'" (Mark 2:5).

"Seeing their faith," Jesus forgave the man. That's a profound picture of the power of *koinonia* fellowship. Sometimes we do not have the faith for our struggles, but when we live differently and live in partnership with others, they can have faith for us when we do not have it ourselves. This is the power of fellowship.

3. *They devoted themselves to the breaking of bread.*

The third principle we find in Acts 2 is that the followers of Jesus rejected a culture of cynicism. One question often asked about this part of the passage is whether Luke uses the phrase "the breaking of the bread" to mean sharing a meal or sharing the sacrament of Communion. My answer is "Yes." I don't mean that to be overly clever, but it's true. Scholars don't agree on which is more accurate.

What *is* clear is that sharing a meal was perhaps the most intimate form of fellowship one could have with fellow believers at the time. In the ancient near eastern world, when a guest was invited to a meal, it was incumbent on the host to provide provision and protection for this guest. Whether this "breaking of the bread" was meant to be a formal worship practice or an informal time of eating together, it definitely reflects a rich life lived together.

Our culture thrives on suspicion, skepticism, and a lack of trust. Just a quick perusal of the daily news or your social media feed will confirm that reality. It's one of the dividing lines I mentioned earlier. Living life together abundantly around the table demolishes this kind of cynicism. Andy Stanley, senior pastor at Northpoint Church in Atlanta writes: "In the absence of information, we get to choose whether we will fill the gap with suspicion or trust." [30] Left to ourselves, we tend to drift towards suspicion and away from trust.

In his best-selling book *The Seven Habits of Highly Effective People*, Stephen Covey tells a story about his own journey from suspicion to trust. One day Covey was on the subway in New York, along with several others. They were sitting quietly, going about their day, when a man boarded the train with his children who were loud and wild. Many of the passengers were irritated, yet the father did nothing. Eventually, Covey confronted the father and asked him if he could take control of his children. Here is how the man responded:

> *The man lifted his gaze as if to come to a consciousness of the situation for the first time and said softly, "Oh, you're right. I guess I should do something about it. We just came from the hospital where their mother died about an hour ago. I don't know what to think, and I guess they don't know how to handle it either."*
>
> *Can you imagine what I felt at that moment? My paradigm shifted. Suddenly I saw things*

differently, and because I saw differently, I thought differently, I felt differently, I behaved differently. My irritation vanished. I didn't have to worry about controlling my attitude or my behavior; my heart was filled with the man's pain. Feelings of sympathy and compassion flowed freely. "Your wife just died? Oh, I'm so sorry! Can you tell me about it? What can I do to help?" Everything changed in an instant. [31]

Like Covey, most of us know our own propensity to fill in the gaps created from an absence of information with suspicion rather than trust. We all are prone to this often-unchecked inclination.

Yet, could we learn from the ancients here? Our spiritual mothers and fathers in the prototype church, like their Hebrew parents before them, understood the power of gathering around a simple table for good food and slow, focused conversation. Whether it was showing hospitality to the stranger or celebrating God's deliverance from Egypt, the ancients understood that food and friendship around a table, with God as an unseen but profoundly present companion, raised trust and lowered suspicion.

Our church has been greatly influenced in recent years by the Fresh Expressions of Church movement that first began among Anglican and Methodist congregations in Britain and has since made its way to America (*www.freshexpressionsus.org; www.freshexpressions.org*). This movement acknowledges that, over time in both Europe and America, the idea of what they call "the third place" has shifted. The first and second places, home and work, have remained the same while the third place, the church, has changed. These places are the primary influences over people's lives. With the increased secularization of our cultures, the local church no longer holds this sacred third place. The new third places—to name a few—are ball fields and coffee shops and gyms and art studios. The Fresh Expressions movement seeks to create new sacred spaces for new people to encounter the gospel.

With this new understanding, Grace Church began to prayerfully consider the places where God is present and where we might encourage faith to arise in new people. As a result, we started to work more in the Suncoast community, a large impoverished area just a few miles from our church. It houses the second largest trailer park in the southeast United States and, on our county food map, is described as being in a "hunger drought." For years, we have served an elementary school in that community, and so we already had relationships with residents and leaders there.

In the fall of 2016, some brave pioneers rented a small, little-used community center in Suncoast to launch a fresh expression of church called "Eat, Pray, Love Dinner Church." This community—filled with generations of women and men, young and old, trapped in cycles of poverty and addiction—welcomed us with open arms.

Every Thursday night our volunteers prepare a meal for our neighbors and sit and talk with them. Over the months, the tables began to pray together. Then a short lesson from the Bible was added to their time together. Sometimes someone would share a testimony. Since its inception in 2016, weddings and funerals have been held there, shoes and backpacks have been distributed, hurricane relief and restoration has occurred, and many people have come to faith in Jesus and been baptized. It all began as a group of people, now friends, coming together to break bread around a table. This is community. This is living differently.

4. They devoted themselves to prayer.

Finally, the first followers of Jesus worked together to reject a culture of self-reliance. The English Standard Version (ESV) is one of the few Bible translations that I believe correctly translates this fourth activity of the prototype church. Most translations translate this word as simply "prayer," but the ESV translates it more literally. In the Greek language, the definitive article "the" is in the sentence and the word "prayer" is actually plural, so this phrase should be translated as: "And they devoted themselves to . . . the prayers" (Acts 2:42, ESV).

Some scholars argue that this means the first followers of Jesus continued to observe the traditional Jewish prayers at the temple. This would make sense because the vast majority of the first Christ-followers were Jewish. We see evidence of this when Luke tells us about Peter and John going to the Temple for the afternoon prayers: "Peter and John went to the Temple one afternoon to take part in the three o'clock prayer service" (Acts 3:1).

Regardless, it is obvious that, in the early days of the Jesus movement, God's people prayed often. So often, in fact, that it is listed as one of the top four things to which they were devoted. God's people, together, were devoted to prayer.

Frankly, as I have studied these texts, I am deeply convicted about both my and my church's lack of prayer. Once again, it points to our rugged individualism and self-reliance. One of the gifts of prayer is that it acknowledges that only God can fix our lives and world. When problems arise, my first instinct is to figure them out on my own. Prayer focuses my life and my circumstances on God.

When we pray, we are admitting we are not ultimately in control of our lives. When we pray, we reject a culture of self-reliance and become "God-reliant" together. Too often we see prayer as a last resort. In fact, most Americans admit this to be true. I've been guilty of this, too. I've thought to myself, *Well, Jorge, you've done all you can . . . so you might as well pray.* A better choice would be to pray and then see if there is anything left to do.

Jesus encouraged us to "ask, seek, and knock," to make our lives and needs known to God. He said to call on God like we would a friend at midnight when there's an emergency. When we have a need, God should be our first resort.

Prayer, however, is not primarily about us going to God; it is also about God coming to us. Prayer involves times of listening too. When we pray, we listen together for God's whisper. Prayer deepens our relationship with God, and we all have a soul-deep need for this relationship.

Also, we all have a soul-deep need to be the object of prayer. It is both affirming and humbling to be on the receiving end of others' prayers. When we allow others to pray for us, we experience the supernatural love of God expressed through our fellow human beings. This love calms us, strengthens us, heals, and lifts us up (James 5:16). Wes Olds, one of my colleagues in ministry at Grace Church, tells a story of being literally lifted up in prayer when he was a self-conscious middle schooler on a youth retreat:

The last night on the retreat, the leaders had the students pray for one another in a unique way. Each person would lay down, then the entire group would physically lift them up and pray for them. This took trust! I watched from the back, thinking this was something the older kids would do without me.

Then I heard my name called. "Wesley, come on dude. We are going to pray for you." I laid down, hoping they wouldn't make fun of me. Then this group picked me up. While I was lifted up, "crowd-surfing" over them all, I heard voices calling out to God on my behalf. These "cool" kids were blessing me as they lifted me up to the Lord.[32]

We need God and we need one another. We are better together when we devote ourselves to this kind of prayer. This was the kind of different living that the prototype church practiced devotedly.

THE JOURNEY INWARD AND THE JOURNEY OUTWARD

So far, in the Scripture we've examined, Luke's description of the prototype church appears pretty inwardly focused. They were passionately committed to the apostles' instructions about the life and ministry of Jesus. They lived in deep and genuine fellowship with one another. They sat at the table eating, lingering, and talking with one another. They prayed together. All the arrows seem to point inward, but the real question is: *What was the result of a life devoted to these practices?*

In Acts 2:43-47, Luke describes the results of this kind of ardent commitment:

A deep sense of awe came over them all, and the apostles performed many miraculous signs and wonders. And all the believers met together in one place and shared everything they had. They sold their property and possessions and shared the money with those in need. They worshiped together at the Temple each day, met in homes for the Lord's Supper, and shared their meals with great joy and generosity—all the while praising God and enjoying the goodwill of all the people. And each day the Lord added to their fellowship those who were being saved.

There is so much here we could focus on, but I want to consider the last line: "And each day the Lord added to their fellowship those who were being saved." These four inward realities led to one staggering outward result. The prototype church had an enduring commitment to four practices that were focused inward but produced an outward life that witnessed to the love of Jesus and resulted in the expansion of Jesus' movement. Their neighborly living led to missional results. These were four missional practices for the first followers of Jesus, and they can be practices for us today as well. Followers of Jesus who neighbor others must themselves also be neighbored well for the movement of Jesus to continue enlarging. So, let's be neighbored and neighbor well.

Questions for Personal Reflection and Group Discussion

1. What does the "agony of defeat" mean to you? When have you experienced the agony of defeat? How has your community helped you during these trying times?

2. What does it mean to say that faithfulness precedes fruitfulness? Where have you seen faithfulness produce fruit in your life?

3. What is the most important takeaway for you from the prototype church? How can these early followers of Jesus inspire you and your church to grow?

4. Do you believe that loneliness and social isolation are an epidemic in our society? If so, what do you think are the causes? How can followers of Christ respond to this problem? What would Jesus do if faced with this situation?

5. What does it mean to live differently? How can we live our lives differently in a way that reflects Jesus? What is one area in particular where you want to focus?

CHAPTER FOUR
A Neighboring Church

If our church disappeared, would the neighborhood know or care?
—Unknown

I have been involved in a pastor's covenant group for more than twenty-eight years. For several of those years Joe, a guy in our group, worked for the Florida Annual Conference of The United Methodist Church. His job was to help the more than eight hundred local churches in the Conference increase their evangelism efforts. Joe visited with local churches, consulted with their leaders, and taught them ways to improve their outreach to the local community.

Most of Joe's work was focused on under-functioning churches in communities with growth potential. His primary method of operation involved arriving early and driving around the church's community while noting local schools, parks, and shopping areas. He would then meet with the leaders and begin with a simple question: *How are your church's evangelism efforts going?*

Joe once told me that the mood in these leadership meetings was often tense. Typically, there was a lot of hemming and hawing. Eventually someone would say something like, "Well, there just aren't any children and families in our neighborhood for us to reach."

It was at this point that Joe would pull out his notes from his pre-meeting expedition, and ask: "What about the local school filled with students that is located six blocks to the north of your church, or the park that is filled with families and located eight blocks south of your church, or the shopping mall that is located three miles from your church?" These questions always preceded a deafening silence in the room.

My colleague at Grace Church, Wes, takes a slightly different approach when meeting with local churches that are struggling with their outreach efforts. Like Joe, he arrives early, but not to map out the places of potential outreach. Instead, Wes arrives early to interview the church's neighbors. I've seen him do this in suburban churches in Southwest Florida and churches in the middle of the slums of Nicaragua. He asks any neighbors who will talk with him, "Hey, do you know what goes on in that building?"—while pointing at the church building.

Some of the responses Wes has heard through the years have been staggering, such as, "We don't know what goes on in that building," a group of brown and black youth on their bikes told Wes, "but on Sundays a bunch of old white people show up." The neighbors of a church located in a barrio in Estelí, Nicaragua, responded to Wes's question with: "Nobody ever shows up at this church unless Americans are visiting. Then the crowds are huge. Other than that, the place sits empty all week." These responses became the fodder for his conversation with the church's leaders later in the week.

Both Joe and Wes were trying to do two things to help churches who seem to have lost their way. First, they were trying to introduce the church to the neighborhood. In so many churches, the people who meet within the walls of the church do not know the neighbors who live outside of them. Secondly, they're both trying to introduce the neighborhood to the church. Sadly, the responses of neighbors in Southwest Florida and Nicaragua are all too common. There is one critical question for local church leaders in these environments to answer: *If our church disappeared, would the neighborhood know or even care?*

THE POWER OF FOCUS

E. Stanley Jones, the great Methodist missionary to India and author of countless books famously wrote: *"Whatever gets your attention gets you."* [33]

We know this is true in our individual lives. If my life becomes centered on the acquisition of wealth or the pursuit of power, money and fame will define me. If instead my life in Christ becomes my focus, then my hunger and thirst for God will define me.

What is true of us as individuals is also true of us as church communities. Whatever gets your congregation's attention becomes the thing that defines your church. In 2009 and 2010, I was privileged to serve on the Call to Action Steering Team for The United Methodist Church. Our goal was to statistically measure the vitality of the more than 32,000 United Methodist churches in the United States of America. It was a daunting task to establish the parameters that allow us to measure local church vitality. After nearly two years of working together and utilizing the expertise of two different consulting organizations, two major reports were released to our denomination. One of the reports reflected on the vitality of our general church (our Council of Bishops and Boards and Agencies), and the other report focused on the vitality of the 32,000 local churches. (The reports of the Call to Action can be found at _www.umc.org/who-we-are/call-to-action_). The results of our study on local churches was staggering. Eighty-five percent of our local churches did not meet the threshold for high vitality based on the four indicators we set.

What was the problem? This was a denomination with the rich heritage of the Wesley brothers and Francis Asbury and Thomas Coke. The early Methodists were highly pragmatic Christian leaders who harnessed the power of community to revolutionize the movement of Jesus in the 1700s in England and the 1800s in America. The gospel was preached to the poor. They established systems of joyful accountability and discipleship and organized ministries for the disadvantaged and marginalized. Yet, sadly, three hundred years later, the vitality of the movement of God through the people called Methodist had become a shadowy remnant of its glorious past.

I would argue that the wisdom of E. Stanley Jones can help our churches. What has our attention in the local church? Far too many of us have taken our corporate gaze off the God who called us to be blessed and be a blessing to the nations (Genesis 12:1-3). In far too many places, the voice of our risen Savior that calls to the people of God has been drowned out by institutional maintenance. The Great Commission has become "the great omission." Like my friends Joe and Wes have discovered firsthand, too many of our churches need to be reintroduced to their neighborhoods, and the neighborhood needs to be reintroduced to the church.

How would our churches be transformed by the Holy Spirit if we redirected our attention to God and

God's mission? What changes would take place if leaders heeded the wisdom offered in the letter to the Hebrews about "fixing our eyes on Jesus" (12:2) and the instruction from Mark's Gospel to "go into all the world and preach the gospel to all creation" (16:15). This kind of focus and attention would be a game changer for every local church.

THE GRACE CHURCH STORY

In the summer of 1996, my bishop sent me to become the new lead pastor at Grace United Methodist Church in the fast-growing community of Cape Coral, Florida. When I arrived, the church was only half-full, but those present were wonderful people. I would describe the church then as having lost its way. The focus of their ministry at the time was simply to keep the doors open. Spaghetti dinners took up lots of time as the members struggled to raise money. This effort took precedence over outreach to the community. It was a life focused on survival.

During my first week, a temporary bookkeeper came into my office and invited me to sit down. She told me that she was not there to give good news. She had spent the previous week balancing the church checkbook and discovered that we had a whopping $29.16 in the checking account. And that wasn't the worst of the news. There was a bank loan for the sanctuary, and a balloon payment was due in a few months. In addition, she said there were unpaid bills totaling $20,000, along with a letter from the Internal Revenue Service regarding unpaid employee taxes. Welcome to Cape Coral, Jorge!

The reality was that the financial condition of the church was also an indicator of the spiritual and missional condition of the congregation. Good people had slowly drifted away from their primary calling to love God and love their neighbors. I love and loathe that line from the hymn "Come Thou Fount of Every Blessing" that goes like this:

Prone to wander, Lord, I feel it,
Prone to leave the God I love.[34]

These words described the missional heart of our congregation. We were adrift and we felt it. Fortunately, a group of about thirty members had recently attended the Walk to Emmaus, a weekend spiritual-life experience and had their "hearts strangely warmed" on their three-day pilgrimage (*www.emmaus. upperroom.org/*).

The Holy Spirit had gone before us once again and, with this small group of leaders and a handful of others, we worked together to regain our focus on Jesus, his mission, and our community.

In those early weeks, I would spend the mornings in prayer asking God for his vision for Grace Church. That fall I boldly announced our new focus to the church: *To partner with God in transforming people from unbelievers to fully devoted disciples of Jesus to the glory of God.*

Of course, this was basically a rewording of the Great Commission that Jesus gave to his disciples before his ascension. With both this new focus and our small team in place, we got busy seeking God's help to live into this lofty picture of our preferred future.

I believe in the power of preaching to help shape the mission of a local church, so for my first nine weeks as pastor, I preached a series called "The Exciting Church." Throughout those nine weeks I planted seeds of faith into the soil of the people called

Grace Church. We spent time studying what the Bible says about God's people and how we are called to love, grow, pray, gather, worship, witness, give, and serve together. Audaciously, we began to envision a future for our church filled with God's Spirit through people who were deeply connected to one another and profoundly committed to loving our neighbors well.

We added a new prayer to our weekly gatherings to help us focus on the neighborhood and God's new vision for Grace Church: "Lord, send us the people nobody else wants." Later, we would add the phrase "and sees" to remind the community that we shared a deep desire to help those who were lost in the dark places of our community. Still today, this prayer drives much of what we do.

By the grace of God our church soon began to grow—some might even say explode. The next eight years was a roller-coaster ride as our average worship attendance grew from 400 to more than 1,500 over four weekly worship services. We added new staff and programs and built a 18,000 square foot children's and youth center to accommodate the influx of students and our weekday preschool. We held large outreach events to introduce the church to the neighborhood and the neighborhood to the church. Our Fall Festival grew from a few hundred attending to thousands of people, our live drama of Jesus' last hours attracted neighbors during Holy Week, and our contemporary worship brought in new young families.

VISITATION COMES IN THE ORDINARY

It was in this season of growth that I learned the power of a simple mantra: *Visitation comes in the ordinary*. Think about Moses. Despite growing up in the palace, Moses encountered God when he was working as a shepherd, having run away from his home after killing an Egyptian solider. Moses had downgraded his life quite a bit when this happened:

One day Moses was tending the flock of his father-in-law, Jethro, the priest of Midian. He led the flock far into the wilderness and came to Sinai, the mountain of God. There the angel of the LORD appeared to him in a blazing fire from the middle of a bush. Moses stared in amazement. Though the bush was engulfed in flames, it didn't burn up (Exodus 3:1-2).

Moses had spent forty years living in the luxury of Pharaoh's palace in Egypt. Then he spent another forty years as a shepherd on the other side of Mount Sinai. After this encounter with God, Moses would spend yet another forty years emancipating God's people from slavery and leading them to the Promised Land.

The timing of this encounter with God is extraordinary. Moses spent day after day, year after year, getting up early to tend to sheep. For forty years, Moses went about his ordinary daily business, and then, out of nowhere, God shows up. No preamble. No extraordinary deed from Moses. God just showed up while Moses was living his life and doing his duty. This same kind of divine invitation to a new life and a new call has happened to me and to the people of Grace Church on several occasions, always calling us to new ways to love our neighbors. I'd like to tell about three of those calls.

MULTISITE MINISTRY

As our church grew in the early 2000s, our biggest problem was space. Our church sat on 6.38 acres and almost an entire acre of that was taken up with water retention and became unusable during our rainy summer months. For years we tried to purchase the property around us to no avail. We also considered relocating to a larger site several miles away, but nothing quite worked out. Then, in 2003, we stumbled upon the emerging multisite movement. This idea finally gave our growing congregation the capacity to influence more neighborhoods in our city. It was a solution that fit like a glove.

Typically, Friday is my day off, but on one particular Friday in 2003, I was driving to our local United Methodist camp to speak at a retreat. As I drove, I passed the Olga-Fort Myers Shores United Methodist Church, and I had my own sort of burning bush moment. I heard a whisper from the Holy Spirit simply say, "I want to do something there." I picked up my cell phone and called my District Superintendent to tell her about this divine visitation in the midst of my ordinary day. In a way that only the Spirit of God can orchestrate, she said she had been praying about this very church in our District and had felt a nudge from the Spirit to talk with me about it. Neither of us was sure what that meant, but we knew that we were both hearing from God. The District Superintendent asked me to continue praying about the situation.

After a few days, we met and I shared with her the idea of Grace Church adopting the Olga-Fort Myers Shores United Methodist Church. This church was located in a wonderful neighborhood filled with old Florida-style homes and population comprised of long-time Floridians, retirees, and an emerging Hispanic and black community. Sadly, the church was in serious decline with a weekly worship attendance of around fifty. Like our congregation in Cape Coral, most of their energy was spent simply trying to keep the doors open.

In January of 2004, my District Superintendent and I met with a small group of leaders from this congregation to see if the adoption idea "seemed good to the Holy Spirit and to us" (Acts 15:28a). The leaders sensed God's affirmation, and one month later, on a Monday night, we held a church conference with 80 people in attendance. By a vote of 70 to 10, the congregation voted to close on July 1, 2004, and become the Fort Myers Shores campus of Grace Church.

In the following months a campus pastor was chosen and the new Fort Myers Shores campus opened. A brave group of neighborhood-loving missionaries returned to their community from the Cape Coral campus to help relaunch this new endeavor and, by God's grace, the campus began to grow rapidly. Fifteen years later, this campus is a vital part of the community with amazing worship, discipleship, and recovery ministries. This neighborhood would indeed know and care if this church vanished.

In the years that have followed, Grace Church has adopted four other United Methodist congregations that were either closing or closed. In time, each site has made the journey from a primarily inward focus to a passionate outward focus on both their immediate neighborhood and the world. This grand experiment has forced us to focus not only on our vision for our church but also on how we can build healthy and holy teams at each campus. The unique contexts of our campuses present their own set of opportunities and challenges, and our strategies for disciple-making and our leadership structures are constantly shifting to meet the needs of each site. Over the years we have spent countless hours wrestling over what each campus needs and where there needs to be continuity across campuses. We do all this because God has given us an assignment to love our neighborhoods in Jesus' name.

OUR GLOBAL NEIGHBORS

Another burning bush moment for our congregation happened in September of 2001. Jan, a remarkable leader in our church, told me the Lord had told her that I was supposed to help her discover her next calling. Jan had previously launched a remarkable ministry in our church but felt like God was calling her to something new. We met month after month and each time she would ask me, "Has the Lord spoken to you about my calling?"

One day, while reading a magazine, I came upon a full-page article about a conference to help local churches create a strategy for global missions. For whatever reason I felt a nudge from the Spirit, tore out the page, and put it on the edge of my desk. I knew I would be meeting with Jan again in a few days, and I knew she would once again ask me that daunting question about her calling. When she walked in a few days later, I slid the article across the desk to her and said, "I think you should go to this." Jan attended the conference and, when she walked into my office the next time, she had an armload of books and a smile on her face. She told me, "Pastor, this is what God has called me to do. He wants me to help awaken Grace Church to her global ministry."

In the weeks after that meeting, Jan and I planned a Global Focus weekend to be led by facilitators from the Mission Society, now called TMS Global, which still helps local churches awaken to global ministry

through Activate Training (*www.tms-global.org*).
Ninety leaders gathered over the weekend to learn
about Jesus' final words to his followers: "But you will
receive power when the Holy Spirit comes upon you.
And you will be my witnesses, telling people about
me everywhere—in Jerusalem, throughout Judea, in
Samaria, and to the ends of the earth" (Acts 1:8).

Over that weekend God broke my heart and the
hearts of our leaders and staff. In response, we began
to intentionally build relationships with mission partners serving around the world. We challenged our
congregation to give beyond their tithes to support
mission partners, go on short-term mission experiences, and pray for our mission partners regularly.

In the seventeen years since, Grace Church has
given millions of dollars to our mission partners and
hundreds of students and adults have joined short-
term mission teams to travel to places like India,
Ghana, Kenya, Cuba, Nicaragua, Costa Rica, and
Mexico. Beyond this we have established relationships
with indigenous pastors and church leaders. They
have been in our homes, and we have been in theirs.
Their neighborhoods have become our neighborhoods. Grace Church now has a global neighborhood
in addition to the neighborhoods of southwest Florida
that we love so dearly.

FROM COME-TO TO GO-TO NEIGHBORS

I'd like to tell one final story about a burning bush
encounter for our congregation. One of the challenges
of serving in the same church for a long time is that
things can become routine. Staying open to the fresh-
wind and fire of the Holy Spirit is a constant challenge
and a sacred chore.

I cut my teeth on a model of evangelism called "the attractional church." In this model, the local church does its best to create an irresistible environment that attracts people to come to us, regardless of their spiritual state. Back in my youth ministry days, this meant planning wacky, crazy events like all-night lock-ins at bowling alleys, video-game establishments, and skating rinks. Students would show up to these events by the hundreds.

When I became a lead pastor of a local church, I went to work implementing adult versions of the same strategies. That meant putting together sermon series that played off of cultural phenomena (like when I based a series of sermons on the reality TV show *Survivor*). It also meant that we shifted from traditional worship services with hymns and creeds and began adding contemporary worship elements like bands and video screens. We did all these things and more to attract new people from our neighborhood into our church.

We were red hot to reach our community in any way we could. That involved presenting more than just worship and discipleship opportunities. Our congregation also organized ministries to the poor, the marginalized, and the addicted of our community. In 2006, we made the decision to buy a vacant grocery store down the street from our original campus in Cape Coral to open the Grace Community Center, a place dedicated to helping people who needed food, vocational training, and various other programs. There was a problem though; the building was expensive. We went to our congregation and told them what we would need. We also told them that if we didn't meet our goals, we would not buy this property. We reached those goals in a few short months and started our work in early 2007.

You may remember that the first signs of the great recession began to show up in 2007, and southwest Florida was one of the first and hardest hit areas in America. We led the nation in home foreclosures, and economic downturn took a serious toll. This was true for our church as well. For the first time in my ten years at Grace Church, our giving went flat and then began to decline, all while we had a hefty new monthly mortgage. But this storm did not stop the amazing people of Grace Church from helping people. As our neighbors began to lose their jobs and homes, we were able to provide food, clothing, medical care, and more at the community center.

It was a noble project, but alas our approach was still a come-to strategy. We were simply inviting our needy neighbors to show up on our doorstep to have their needs met. Throughout the recession, we served more than 250,000 people, and hundreds prayed to receive Christ as their Savior during this season. But after much research, we discovered that very few actually were integrated into our congregation. Could it be that our come-to strategy wasn't actually working to make new disciples for Jesus?

After ten years we shut down and sold the Grace Community Center and moved all of the ministries housed there to new locations, mostly outside of our church. A few of the larger ministries leased new space in a strip mall. Feeding ministries moved to a nearby community center and a local elementary school. Slowly we pivoted from being a come-to outreach effort to a go-to strategy. The results have been inspiring.

By moving our ministries into the community, we have built long-term, genuine relationships with our neighbors. From the elementary school staff to the families who show up with their children, Grace Church has built a relationship of integrity, like Jesus, because we moved into the neighborhood (John 1:14, MSG).

GREATER THINGS

'The person who trusts me will not only do what I'm doing but even greater things, because I, on my way to the Father, am giving you the same work to do that I've been doing. You can count on it" (John 14:12, MSG).

These can be intimidating words for any serious follower of Jesus. I know they are for me. It doesn't take a deep examination of the Gospels to notice Jesus doing some pretty amazing stuff. He walked on water, raised the dead, and fed thousands with one boy's lunch. Jesus cast out demons and quieted storms with a word. We're going to do "greater things" than this? Those are some high expectations.

I believe in miracles and I believe they still happen today, but these powerful moments are rare. Even the most gifted healer can't replicate the healing power of Jesus. Nobody measures up to Jesus, but Jesus didn't say, "If you trust in yourself, you'll be able to do amazing things." He said, "The person who trusts me will not only do what I'm doing but even greater things."

So where are these greater things? Do we lack faith? Do we just not trust God enough? I don't think that's the case. I think the issue is that we misunderstand the mission of Jesus. Think about these questions: Why did Jesus come to earth? Was it primarily to demonstrate the power of God? I don't believe it was. I think the Bible teaches us that Jesus came to this sin-sick planet not to flex God's muscles but to show us God's heart. Jesus didn't come to show off God's power but to show us God's love! Every miracle and every demonstration of power was motivated by love.

Why did Jesus raise Jarius' daughter from the dead? (Mark 5:35-43). To demonstrate the Father's love for all his children. Why did he feed the hungry crowds? (Matthew 14:13-21; Mark 6:31-44; Luke 9:12-17; John 6:1-14). To show that God loves God's children and provides for them. Jesus' miracles were done with a greater goal in mind—to help us know that God loves us!

Here's the deal. I think the greater things Jesus mentions in this verse are all about demonstrating, embodying, and expressing God's love to people. This is what the body of Christ is called to do. These are the "greater things" we will do if we trust in Jesus. Embodying God's love is the primary task of followers of Jesus. It is the primary reason the local church exists.

Recently, Taylor, one of our staff members, felt a nudge from the Holy Spirit to start a new ministry on Sunday morning. Taylor came to me one day and said, "Jorge, I'd like permission to be gone on Sunday mornings, to go and see where Aslan is on the move." Aslan is the Christlike character in C.S. Lewis' famous *Chronicles of Narnia* series. Now, I'm a pastor so Sunday mornings are pretty important to me. My first thought was, *Why in the world do you have to do this on Sunday morning? Aren't there other times to do this? Plus, you'll miss out on my great preaching!* Thankfully, the better angels of my nature intervened, and I responded, "Sure, go see where Jesus is on the move and report back."

After a few weeks on her Spirit-led expedition, Taylor reported she had found a perfect place for our church to showcase the love of Jesus. In her work,

Taylor had been joined by a Spanish-speaking couple from our church, and they had discovered a flea market frequented by the local Latino community on Sunday mornings. The team rented a space, set up a few t-shirts for sale, offered free face painting, and posted a sign in Spanish and English advertising, "Free Prayer Here."

Over the period of a few months, Aslan did indeed show up. Through the efforts of this amazing team, people were prayed for and healed. Spiritual conversations took place, and the light of Jesus began to push back the darkness of the devil in the lives of many. This may seem like a small thing, but it's one of the "greater things" Jesus mentioned. It's an example of God's love present in the world.

THE STORY OF THE GOOD NEIGHBOR

One of the best biblical illustrations of this love is found in the well-known parable of the good Samaritan. The context of this story is important to understand it:

One day an expert in religious law stood up to test Jesus by asking him this question: "Teacher, what should I do to inherit eternal life?" Jesus replied, "What does the law of Moses say? How do you read it?" The man answered, "'You must love the Lord your God with all your heart, all your soul, all your strength, and all your mind.' And, 'Love your neighbor as yourself.'" "Right!" Jesus told him. "Do this and you will live!" The man wanted to justify his actions, so he asked Jesus, "And who is my neighbor?" (Luke 10:25-29).

Keep in mind as we work through this story that Jesus is telling this story to a religious man. He is looking for an answer to an honorable question, "What should I do to inherit eternal life?" In response, Jesus does what he so often does. He answers a question with a question. "What does the Torah, the law of Moses say?" Like a good student of the Torah, the questioning man answers, "Love God with all that you are. Love your fellow man as you love yourself." This was Judaism 101!

Then comes an intriguing twist. "The man wanted to justify his actions, so he asked Jesus, 'And who is my neighbor?'" The question feels like a bit of a ruse, doesn't it? You can hear the internal monologue: "I'm a good guy! I go to the synagogue. I tithe." Jesus has answered his question, but he wants one final sign-off to prove to himself that he's on the right path. What he doesn't realize is that Jesus wants more than that, he wants his heart. Jesus answers his second question with a story:

A Jewish man was traveling from Jerusalem down to Jericho, and he was attacked by bandits. They stripped him of his clothes, beat him up, and left him half dead beside the road. By chance a priest came along. But when he saw the man lying there, he crossed to the other side of the road and passed him by. A Temple assistant walked over and looked at him lying there, but he also passed by on the other side. Then a despised Samaritan came along, and when he saw the man, he felt compassion for him (Luke 10:30-33).

If you're the man listening to Jesus, this story starts off fine. A Jewish traveler is beaten and left for dead by bandits. That's sad, but not uncommon in that day. This was a serious threat when traveling alone. Also, it wasn't a big deal that the priest or the temple assistant did not help the traveler. If they did, they would be made unclean and would be unable to do their important religious work. The air would have been sucked out of the room, however, when Jesus introduced the man who did help the beaten traveler.

"Then a despised Samaritan came along . . .." You can feel everyone who's listening tighten up. There was a long-standing feud between Jews and Samaritans. This is like Gators and Seminoles in college football or North Carolina and Duke in college basketball. There is no love lost here. Yet, Jesus tells us that the Samaritan had compassion on the injured man.

The Greek word Jesus uses here is *splagchnizomai*. It means "to feel sympathy, to pity, or to be moved with compassion" (*www.blueletterbible.org/lang/lexicon/lexicon.cfm?t=kjv&strongs=g4697*). The word is used twelve times in the New Testament, mostly in reference to Jesus' feelings toward others. Compassion was a deeply felt emotion that led Jesus to action. When Jesus was filled with compassion, healing words and actions often followed. Henri J.M. Nouwen wrote about the responsibilities of compassion for Christ-followers:

Compassion asks us to go where it hurts, to enter into places of pain, to share in brokenness, fear, confusion, and anguish. Compassion challenges us to cry out with those in misery, to mourn with those who are lonely, to weep with those in tears. Compassion requires us to be weak with the weak, vulnerable with the vulnerable, and powerless with the powerless. Compassion means full immersion in the condition of being human.[35]

This kind of compassion is what we see from the Samaritan in Jesus' story. What he does next models for us what it means to truly love our neighbor. He puts his compassion into action.

HOW DO WE LOVE OUR NEIGHBORS WELL?

There are two concrete ways the good Samaritan loved his neighbor in this story, and they are also ways we, as followers of Jesus, can love our neighbors today.

1. We love our neighbors well by giving immediate aid.

Going over to him, the Samaritan soothed his wounds with olive oil and wine and bandaged them. Then he put the man on his own donkey and took him to an inn, where he took care of him (Luke 10:34).

In Jesus' story, the compassionate, neighborly Samaritan finds a man beaten and battered on the side of the road. What does he first do? He literally and figuratively stops the bleeding. He gives immediate aid to stop the crisis the traveler was experiencing. In this story, doing so involves a bit of rudimentary EMT work. The Samaritan loaded the beaten man into a first-century ambulance (a donkey) and took him to a medical facility (an inn). The beaten man did not need a sermon on why traveling alone is a bad idea or how he could travel more safely next time. He needed someone to end the nightmare. He needed help.

Ask yourself these questions about your church:

- How does my church reflect the love of Jesus for people in immediate need of help?
- Do we do anything to "stop the bleeding"?
- What basic human needs can our church address?

The answers to these questions come in a variety of forms. It might be a food bank, a clothes closet, or a medical ministry. Whatever it is, the first priority to help people is to end the crisis.

2. We love our neighbors well by giving long-term support.

The next day he handed the innkeeper two silver coins, telling him, "Take care of this man. If his bill runs

higher than this, I'll pay you the next time I'm here"
(Luke 10:35).

The Samaritan stops the bleeding, then takes him to an inn and arranges for him to have a room. If we're honest, a lot of us would think that the Samaritan's responsibility for the beaten man ended here. The short-term crisis is over. But is that truly what it means to love your neighbor as you love yourself? The Samaritan goes even further. He commits himself financially and covers the man's need for further recovery. He essentially says, "Here's my credit card, cover whatever he needs." He wants to help the man move on and regain his independence.

Again, ask yourself what your church does to help people in this way.

- Is your church engaged in long-term relationships with its neighbors?

- In what ways does your church invest in broken and hurting people to help lift them from their despair?

- How is your community helping others move from dependence to independence?

Once again, there are a lot of possibilities. Some might include GED class, English as a second language courses, parenting groups, recovery groups. It's not about the specific ministry; it's about helping your neighbors and supporting them with what they need in the long run.

AID AND ADVANCEMENT THROUGH RECOVERY

For more than eighteen years, Grace Church has been deeply invested in helping people recover from their addictions and compulsive behaviors (*www.egracechurch.com/recovery*). Our ministry works with those recovering from drugs and alcohol, but over the years has grown to include those recovering from overeating, sexual addiction, codependency, nicotine, anger, as well as physical, emotional, and sexual abuse. On a weekly basis, we see between 300 to 400 people at our five campuses for Christ-centered recovery meetings, and we host another 600 to 700 for traditional 12-step meetings.

Particularly when it comes to drugs and alcohol, it's not unusual for someone to walk into one of our meetings under the influence and in desperate need of help. This is not the time for a sermon on the evils of drugs and alcohol—that simply won't help in the moment. Instead, our job is to come alongside this precious child of God with immediate aid. Typically, with the help of our recovery partners in the community, we work to get this person into treatment as soon as possible. We also send a team every Thursday to the 72-hour detox center to offer a 12-step meeting. This is our way to help stop the bleeding through immediate aid.

But, as I said before, the work doesn't end once the short-term crisis is over. We offer 12-step meetings seven days a week at one of our campuses. Two large Christ-centered meetings are held each week, and they are the centerpiece of our recovery ministry. At these gatherings, participants are encouraged to take part in step studies that help them go deeper in their recovery with a smaller group. These studies also encourage the formation of sponsor relationships which are important for accountability. These meetings are our best efforts to provide long-term support for those in recovery.

MARKS OF A GOOD NEIGHBOR

After finishing his story about the good Samaritan,

Jesus turns to the man who inspired the story and asks one more piercing question:

"Now which of these three would you say was a neighbor to the man who was attacked by bandits?" Jesus asked. The man replied, "The one who showed him mercy" (Luke 10:36-37a).

Jesus lifts up the hated and despised Samaritan as the hero of the parable. The "zero" in Jesus' story becomes the hero. Jesus basically said, "This guy gets noticed by God because he was a good neighbor."

Giving immediate aid and long-term support were vital in the first century and they are vital today. This is how we love our neighbors well. In February 1994, Mother Teresa spoke these powerful words at the National Prayer Breakfast in Washington, D.C.:

It is not enough for us to say: "I love God," but I also have to love my neighbor. St. John says that you are a liar if you say you love God and you don't love your neighbor. How can you love God whom you do not see, if you do not love your neighbor whom you see, whom you touch, with whom you live? And so it is very important for us to realize that love, to be true, has to hurt. I must be willing to give whatever it takes not to harm other people and, in fact, to do good to them. This requires that I be willing to give until it hurts. Otherwise, there is not true love in me and I bring injustice, not peace, to those around me. It hurt Jesus to love us. We have been created in His image for greater things, to love and to be loved. [36]

Mother Teresa is right! We are created in God's image for greater things. When we trust in Jesus, we can embody God's love and share it with others.

The late Brennan Manning once wrote:

If indeed we lived a life in imitation of his, our witness would be irresistible. If we dared to live beyond our self-concern; if we refused to shrink from being vulnerable; if we took nothing but a compassionate attitude toward the world; if we were a counterculture to our nation's lunatic lust for pride of place, power, and possessions; if we preferred to be faithful rather than successful, the walls of indifference to Jesus Christ would crumble. A handful of us could be ignored by society; but hundreds, thousands, millions of such servants would overwhelm the world. [37]

When the people of God join Jesus in loving their neighbors well, it's a game changer. People who love their neighbors well change their churches; churches filled with these people change their communities; and communities of these people change the world. When they disappear, people notice.

One last thing about the story. After the man hesitantly admits to Jesus that the despised Samaritan was the good neighbor, Jesus adds a finishing flourish on his message. It's a powerful word for every follower of Jesus and every local church: "Then Jesus said, 'Yes, now go and do the same'" (Luke 10:37b).

Friends, this is the charge of our Master—to go and love our neighbors well. Throughout the whole world, the cry of our neighbors truly is: "Please won't you be my neighbor?" [38]

Questions for Personal Reflection and Group Discussion

1. What do you think about the statement, "Whatever gets your attention gets you?" What attracts your attention in life? What do you think has the attention of your church?

2. What does it mean to say "visitation comes in the ordinary"? How has the Holy Spirit spoken to you in the ordinary moments of your life?

3. What is the difference between a come-to and go-to ministry? How can we shift our focus from one type of ministry to the other?

4. What do you think Jesus means when he says we will do greater things? What are some examples of greater things that you think followers of Jesus are doing in the world today?

5. How do you see your local church putting into practice the two ways to love your neighbors well? How does your church give immediate aid or long-term support? In what areas can you help your church improve?

ENDNOTES

1 From "Won't You Be My Neighbor," 1990; WORDS: Fred M. Rogers. ©McFeely-Rogers Foundation. All rights reserved.

2 From Presbyterian Historical Society. "Remembering Mr. Rogers." *www.history.pcusa.org/blog/remembering-mr-rogers*. (accessed March 4, 2019).

3 From "Won't You Be My Neighbor," by Fred M. Rogers.

4 From *The Seven Habits of Highly Effective People*, by Stephen R. Covey (Simon & Schuster, 2013); page 154.

5 From English translations of The Nicene Creed © 1988 English Language Liturgical Consultation (ELLC). www.englishtexts.org. Used by permission.

6 From *The Lion, the Witch and the Wardrobe* (Chronicles of Narnia Series #2), by C.S. Lewis (Harper Collins Publishers, 2004); page 146.

7 Adapted from *Children of the Second Birth*, by Sam Shoemaker (Fleming H. Revell, 1927); page 25.

8 From *www.umcmission.org/Find-Resources/John-Wesley-Sermons/The-Wesleys-and-Their-Times/The-Character-of-a-Methodist*

9 From *Five Marks of a Methodist*, by Steve Harper (Abingdon Press, 2015).

10 See *https://www.apnews.com/0171876a46b295c3e297b8b4baad20bf*

11 From *The Works of the Rev. John Wesley, A.M.*, an Extract from June 10, 1785; page 620.

12 From *www.christianitytoday.com/history/people/denominationalfounders/john-wesley.html* (accessed May 6, 2019).

13 From *www.ccel.org/ccel/wesley/journal.vi.ii.xvi.html* (accessed May 5, 2019)

14 From *www.ccel.org/ccel/wesley/journal.vi.iii.i.html?highlight=saturday,march,31,1739#highlight* (accessed May 6, 2019)

15 From *www.ccel.org/ccel/wesley/journal.*

16 Discussed in *Acts for Everyone, Part 2,* by Nicolas Thomas Wright (John Knox Press: 2008); page 81.

17 From "Hosanna," words and music by Brooke Fraser (Hosanna Lyrics @ Capital Christian Music Group, 2007); *www.hillsong.com/lyrics/hosanna/* (accessed May 6, 2019).

18 From *The Wounded Healer*, by Henri J.M. Nouwen (Image Books, 1979); page xvi.

19 From Deb Hirsch (Sermon at Missio Ecclesia, Grace Church, February 18, 2016).

20 From *A Beautiful Mess*, by Danielle Strickland (Lion Hudson, 2014); page 16.

21 From *A Beautiful Mess*, Strickland, 16.

22 Adapted from *A Grace Full Life*, by Jorge Acevedo and Wes Olds (Abingdon Press, 2017); pages 38-40.

23 From "Anything Short of Sin" Message Series, by Craig Groeschel at Life Church (January 2015); *www.life.church/talkitover/jesus-and-we-4.*

24 From *https://www.umcmission.org/Find-Resources/John-Wesley-Sermons/The-Wesleys-and-Their-Times/Advice-to-a-People-Called-Methodist*

25 From *www.barna.com/research/sharing-faith-increasingly-optional-christians/*

26 From *The Works of John Wesley, Preface to Poetical Works*, by John Wesley (Hendrickson Publishers, 1991); page 321.

27 Discussed at *https://kinginstitute.stanford.edu/king-papers/documents/ drum-major-instinct-sermon-delivered-ebenezer-baptist-church*

28 From *A Simple Path: Mother Teresa*, by Mother Teresa (Ballantine Books, 1995); page 79.

29 From *Making All Things New: An Invitation to the Spiritual Life*, by Henri Nouwen (HarperCollins, 2009); pages 32-33.

30 From *Trust Versus Suspicion: How to Create and Maintain a Culture of Trust in Your Organization*, by Andy Stanley; *https://itunes.apple.com/podcast/ andy-stanley-leadership-podcast/id290055666?mt=2*

31 From *The Seven Habits of Highly Effective People*, Covey, 30-31.

32 From Rev. Wes Olds (Sermon, Grace Church, Cape Coral, FL, September 29-30, 2018).

33 From *The Way*, by E. Stanley Jones (Abingdon Press, 2015); page 96.

34 From "Come Thou Fount of Every Blessing"; WORDS: Robert Robinson, 1758, based on 1 Samuel 7:12.

35 From *Compassion: A Reflection on the Christian Life*, by Henri J.M. Nouwen; Donald P. McNeill; and Douglas A. Morrison (Image, 2006); pages 3-4.

36 From Mother Teresa, The National Prayer Breakfast (speech, Washington, DC, February 1994); *www.priestsforlife.org/brochures/mtspeech.ht*.

37 From *The Signature of Jesus: The Call to a Life Marked by Holy Passion and Relentless Faith*, by Brennan Manning (Multnomah Books, 1996); pages 44-45.

38 From "Won't You Be My Neighbor," 1990; WORDS: Fred M. Rogers. ©McFeely-Rogers Foundation. All rights reserved.

OTHER BIBLE TRANSLATIONS USED

CPSIA information can be obtained
at www.ICGtesting.com
Printed in the USA
LVHW021506270619
622534LV00002B/2/P

9 781501 877605